OPEN ROAD'S BEST OF

The **Florida Keys & Everglades**

by Bruce Morris

OPEN ROAD TRAVEL GUIDES –
designed for the amount of time you *really* have for your trip!

Open Road Publishing

Open Road's new travel guides.
Designed to cut to the chase.
You don't need a huge travel encyclopedia – you need a *selective guide* to steer you right. If you're going on vacation for a few weeks or less, get a guide that brings you the *best* of any destination for the amount of time you *really* have for your trip!

Open Road – the guide you need for the trip you want.

The New Open Road *Best Of* Travel Guides.
Right to the point.
Uncluttered.
Easy.

4th Edition

OPEN ROAD PUBLISHING
P.O. Box 284, Cold Spring Harbor, NY 11724
www.openroadguides.com

Text Copyright © 2012 by Bruce Morris
- All Rights Reserved -
ISBN 13: 978-1-59360-166-9
ISBN 10: 1-59360-166-2
Library of Congress Control No. 2012933003

About the Author
Bruce Morris grew up in Miami, and is now a writer and musician. He lives in Oak Ridge, Tennessee and at Lake Atitlán in Guatemala. Visit his website, *www.brucemorris.com*, to learn more about Bruce and view his photos from around the world.

For photo credits and acknowledgments, turn to page 223.

Contents

Maps

1. INTRODUCTION

The **Florida Keys** are a semi-tropical paradise. A wide variety of attractions are here: sun, sand, coral reefs, delicious game fish, brilliantly colored ocean and spectacular scenery. The Keys are also one of the country's most popular party spots. There are loads of great restaurants, wild bars, and nightclubs bursting with alternative lifestyle types. There are plenty of things to do during the day and at night and, for the most part, prices are not yet sky-high.

Some visitors come for the sun and sea, some come for the suds and sin. It's a famously lifestyle-tolerant area so you can be yourself without fear of ridicule. It's not a particularly expensive place to visit and is remarkably undeveloped—there are few cheesy tourist attractions and very few high-rise condo towers blocking the view of the beach.

One of the best things about the Keys is that is a warm, semi-tropical paradise within the USA. You can drive your car here from Wichita if you like.

If nightlife is your thing, Key West is calling you. If you like the outdoors and life on the water, the relatively untouched reefs and thousands of mangrove islets in Florida Bay are ready and waiting.

2. OVERVIEW

The Keys are a place to relax. The Keys are a place to party. The Keys are a place to get close to nature and enjoy the only living coral reef in the continental United States. The Keys are a place for sailing, fishing, scuba diving, zooming around on personal watercraft, kayaking, snorkeling, and water-skiing.

The Keys are many things to many people. Your holiday time there is what you want to make it. Whether you are a nerdy bird watcher or a rowdy spring breaker, you'll find what you're looking for in the Keys.

This book is divided into four different touring regions. This chapter briefly describes the delights of each region and suggests a few itineraries.

KEY LARGO & THE UPPER KEYS

Famous for **Bogart, Bacall** and **booze**, Key Largo and the **Upper Keys** have all the goodies the region is famous for. The scuba diving and snorkeling are justly world-famous, as is the fishing for bonefish, tarpon, snapper, wahoo, dorado and sailfish. One of the world's great outdoor experiences is poking around in the mangrove keys and the sand and turtle grass flats in a small boat or kayak. Exotic sea creatures abound in the waters around these sunny keys.

The first key you reach after driving through the bit of Everglades south of Homestead is **Key Largo**. It's a long key. US 1 is the only main road as it heads southwest towards Key West. There is a strip of businesses along both sides of the highway with small motels, luxurious resorts, dive shops, T-shirt joints, seafood restaurants, fast food emporiums, and a few places set up primarily for the enjoyment of **tropical adult beverages**.

To the north of Key Largo lie the

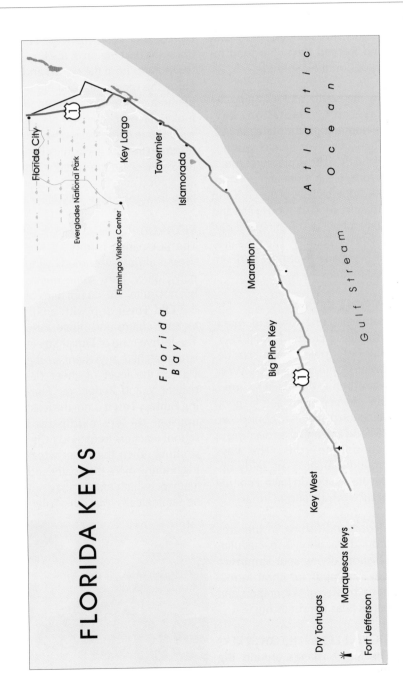

FLORIDA KEYS

Atlantic Ocean

Gulf Stream

Florida Bay

Everglades National Park

Flamingo Visitors Center

Florida City

Key Largo

Tavernier

Islamorada

Marathon

Big Pine Key

Key West

Dry Tortugas

Marquesas Keys

Fort Jefferson

rarely visited **Rhodes, Elliot, Sand** and **Ragged Keys**. No road intrudes on their solitude.

To the south of Key Largo lie **Tavernier, Plantation Key, Islamorada** and the **Matecumbes**. These offer even quieter versions of the usual Keys pleasures: quiet resorts, clean mom-and pop motels, superb views of the Gulf and Atlantic, good seafood to eat, and some of the best fishing and diving in the country. The pleasures of **Everglades National Park** are just minutes away.

MIDDLE KEYS

Between Long Key and Marathon lies a chain of small keys. The only town of any size between Homestead and Key West, **Marathon** is the place to find a big grocery store and a good selection of places to honk down seafood and enjoy an evening of sounds and suds. The keys around Marathon are fairly undeveloped but do have a couple of nice resorts and marinas.

Diving and fishing in the area around Marathon is spectacular. Offshore diving spot **Sombrero Key** is famous for coral formations the size of skyscrapers and barracudas almost as big.

BIG PINE KEY & THE LOWER KEYS

The larger islands around **Big Pine** offer little in the way of commercial conveniences, but this is the best region of the Keys to get away from the crowd and enjoy the spectacular sea life in the area. There are a couple of funky places to stay and eat, as well as one of the top ten luxury resorts in the US. It's a quick hop to Key West, so the Lower Keys are a good area to use as a quiet base for a long Keys holiday.

KEY WEST

The fascinating history of Key West is almost subsumed by the party, party, party atmosphere, but not quite. The quaint parts of the **Old Town** drip with architectural charm and pirate lore. The festive tone of **Duval Street** is unmatched anywhere in the US for the level of sheer debauchery and hedonism. During **Fantasy Fest** it is not the least unusual to see middle-aged school teachers from Sioux City strutting down the street wearing nothing more than paint and feathers (which may or may not be strategically placed). Toler-

ance is the norm. **Gays flock to Key West's permissive scene** knowing they will be free to act like anyone else on holiday without being persecuted.

Nearby **Fort Jefferson** in the **Dry Tortugas** is a great day trip by high-speed catamaran.

EVERGLADES NATIONAL PARK

The third largest park in the lower 48, **Everglades National Park** (*see photo below*) covers about 2500 square miles of primeval wilderness. Wildlife viewing combined with peaceful water sports, interpretive walking and paddling trails, pontoon boat tours and fishing the labyrinth of **Ten Thousand Islands** entertain visitors.

NIGHTLIFE & ENTERTAINMENT

The Florida Keys offer a vast variety of bars, nightclubs and places to have fun. Live music is common throughout the Keys, although it tends more toward alcohol-fueled sing-alongs than sophisticated artistry. The pinnacle of Keys nightlife is **Key West**, which is notorious around the world for its non-stop party. From the nightly festival on Mallory Square to the rowdy bars of Duval Street to yearly events such as Bike Week and Fantasy Fest, Key West offers endless excuses to drink, shout, and run around acting crazy.

FOOD & DRINK

Keys cuisine is famous for its innovative use of **local seafood**. Fish, shrimp and other ocean

creatures are fresh and delicious. Innovative chefs fuse Asian, tropical and local culinary influences. Yellowtail and hog snapper are particularly delicious. A **margarita** is the perfect drink to get you in a tropical mood.

Unfortunately, due to the undiscerning taste of most tourists, many establishments serve up bland, overpriced frozen seafood, and margaritas made with powdered mixes rather than with actual limes. Many bars squirt their margaritas and daiquiris out of plastic hoses just like coke or sprite—it's just a different button on the nozzle. Don't let this bother you. After the first three drinks, none of this is important. Plastic cups are the norm.

DIVING & SNORKELING
The Keys have the most spectacular **coral reefs** in the US. A rainbow of coral and tropical fish awaits you. A very well developed dive industry makes it easy to plan the dive vacation of a lifetime. Many reefs are in shallow water, just a short way offshore, so the wonders of the undersea world are easily accessible to **snorkelers** too. Even if you've never snorkeled before, you simply must give it a try before you leave the Keys.

FISHING
The Keys have a huge variety of fishing opportunities. Inside Florida Bay are vast expanses of sand **flats and turtle grass**, perfect territory for bonefish, permit and tarpon. Silver kings that average 40-80 pounds will trash your tackle with astonishing leaps into the air. The **reefs** hold snapper, grouper and jacks – you might bring home a couple of yellowtail snapper for the grill. **Offshore** anglers battle with sailfish, wahoo, dorado, tuna, kingfish and shark. The waters around the **mangroves** and **backcountry** keys are stiff with snook.

ATTRACTIONS
The Keys have their roadside attractions, though not so many as other touristed areas of the US. Some are high quality and interesting and some are cheesy. Gawk at **pirate treasure**, swim with **dolphins**, marvel at the statue of a **giant Florida crawfish** or tour **Hemingway's old Key West home**. There are plenty of these types of attractions for

all ages. Bring sunscreen, water and your fanny pack.

BIRD WATCHING

With over one hundred (and counting) bird species available for viewing, it's impossible for even the most hard-core birder to visit the Keys without adding significantly to their life list. Acrobatic **roseate terns** and **sharp-shinned hawks**, along with a wide assortment of LBBs (Little Brown Birds), flit through the scrub, and vast flocks of **shore birds** patrol the waterfront. If the birding gods smile on you, you may even see a rare **white ibis**, a **mangrove cuckoo**, or a **black-whiskered vireo**. **Fort Jefferson** in the Dry Tortugas is a holy destination for even the most dedicated of international twitchers.

BEACHES, PARKS & ECO-WALKS

The Keys are not famous for nice sandy beaches. The beaches in the Keys tend to be of the "interesting" variety, with coral, coarse sand, and lots of stuff washed up in heaps. **Smathers Beach** in Key West, **Bahía Honda State Park** and **Cocoplum** in Marathon are about the nicest. Waves are almost always very small. The offshore reefs break up heavy surf long before it reaches land. Snorkeling is the thing to do at Keys beaches—not surfing.

KAYAKING

The Key's mangrove islets and hundreds of square miles of sand and turtle grass flats are made for kayaking. A kayak is an excellent way to explore the lagoons and mangrove wetlands of the

FLORIDA KEYS & EVERGLADES FACTOIDS

Location:	Southern Tip of Florida
Elevation:	5 feet, 43 feet at top of the landfill
Population:	80,000
Climate:	Semi-tropical
Average Temperature:	January 68°, August 83°
Rainfall:	January 2.4 inches, August 6 inches
Major Airports:	Miami, Key West

Keys, or the grass flats out on Florida Bay. Kayak fishing is a growing new sport catered to by many Keys outfitters.

TAKING THE KIDS

You'll find attractions specially aimed at kids, and most tourist areas of the Keys have organized tours and activities appropriate for the whole family. Many lodging places have larger rooms available for family groups. Burgers, chicken, fried potatoes and other kid-friendly food is not hard to find. **Tropical fruits** are a special treat!

3. THE UPPER KEYS

HIGHLIGHTS

▲ Walking the old bridges and deserted beaches

▲ Kayak tour through the mangroves

▲ John Pennekamp Coral Reef State Park

▲ Flats & Reef Fishing

▲ All-you-can-eat seafood fests

INTRO

The **Upper Keys** are a quick hop by car from Miami—good for a day trip—and have almost all of the fun things to do and see the Keys are famous for. For drunken nudity and hard partying you'll

COORDINATES

Key Largo is the largest key in the **Upper Keys.** It's an easy couple of hours drive from Miami. **Everglades National Park** borders the bay side and **John Pennekamp Coral Reef State Park** is on the ocean side. The Upper Keys run from **Ragged Key** to **MM 60.**

have to go on down the road another 100 miles or so to Key West.

The Upper Keys are more for **relaxing** and **exploring nature**, above and underwater. But don't worry – there are plenty of places to swallow beer and fruit-flavored rum drinks when it's time to party.

Only an hour or so from Miami, the Upper Keys are a great place to enjoy water sports, relax poolside, quietly contemplate nature and indulge in great seafood. There are several quiet waterfront resorts to choose from.

The Upper Keys are convenient to Miami for a day trip by car. It's only 60 miles to Key Largo from the Miami airport. If the traffic gods smile on you, you can get from downtown Miami to Key Largo in a couple of hours. See *Practical Matters* for the best route out of town.

THE UPPER KEYS IN A DAY

A few miles past Homestead and the end of the Florida Turnpike, the route to the Keys splits. Take the route that goes through **Card Sound** to Key Largo so you can stop at **Alabama Jack's** for a few beers or rum concoctions and some crab cakes, getting into the proper Keys mood. The Card Sound route involves a minor $1.50 toll, and takes a little longer, but you do get to have a quick one at Jack's.

Be sure your designated driver refrains from the enjoyment of alcoholic beverages at this point.

You'll pass **Crocodile Lake National Wildlife Refuge**

SIGHTS

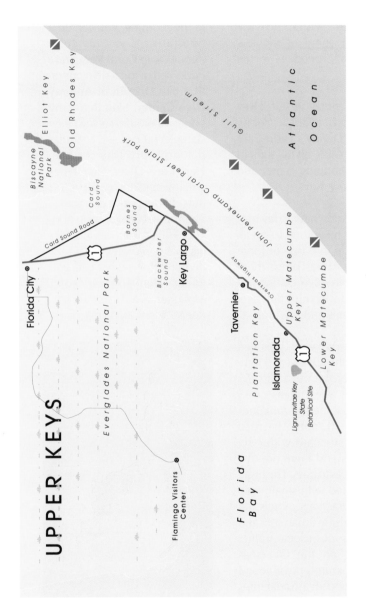

UPPER KEYS

Florida City

Everglades National Park

Flamingo Visitors Center

Florida Bay

Biscayne National Park

Elliot Key

Old Rhodes Key

Card Sound Road

Card Sound

Barnes Sound

Blackwater Sound

Key Largo

Gulf Stream

John Pennekamp Coral Reef State Park

Atlantic Ocean

Tavernier

Plantation Key

Overseas Highway

Islamorada

Upper Matecumbe Key

Lower Matecumbe Key

Lignumvitae Key State Botanical Site

SIGHTS

which is mostly mangroves and scrub which provide cover for some of the few American Crocodiles in the US.

Once you find yourself in **Key Largo**, grab a quick Cuban coffee at **Denny's Latin Café** at MM 100 BS, on the right in a small shopping center and start to have fun.

If you are down for a day trip, you only have time to break the day up into two or three activities. At least one of them needs to involve getting out on the water to enjoy the spectacular reefs and sea life.

Drive Slowwwww! The speed limit on the Overseas Highway is, for the most part, 55 mph with a few areas of 45 mph and some school zones down to 30 mph. The road has long stretches with only two lanes and there are few good places to pass. The highway is lined with small businesses, attractions, motels and other roadside urban stuff and there is a lot of local traffic. Hurrying on the Overseas Highway is rarely possible and never a good idea. Radar traps are common.

Morning

In the morning, you can do a two-tank dive at **John Pennekamp Coral Reef State Park**, with a local dive operation like **Dive In** or **Amoray Dive Center**. Skip the corny underwater *Christ of the Deep* statue. You can see a similar statue on dry land for free. Hard-core Diver Dan types will love the huge wrecks just outside the park boundaries. The *Spiegel Grove, Benwood, USS Alligator* and several others make for weeks of wreck diving if that's what gets you going. *Hen and Chickens, Molasses, French and Pickles Reefs* are famous dive choices.

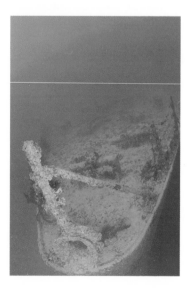

Kayaking through the mangroves and over the turtle grass flats is one eco activity all visitors to the Keys should appreciate. This is a good way to get an up-close look at bird nesting sites, sharks, stingrays, sea urchins, crabs, Florida crawfish and all manner of blowfish and other strange critters. Several outfitters, such as **Robbie's**, can get you on the water and lead you on a guided tour of **Indian Key** and the surrounding flats.

Have lunch at **Ballyhoo's** in the center median on Key Largo. They usually have an all-you-can-eat special on stone crab claws for around $35. It's just a little place in the highway median but they *always* have great seafood.

Afternoon

If you must swim with those loveable **dolphins**, there are several places you can indulge yourself in this more-or-less socially acceptable form of animal abuse. Captive, coerced dolphins are available for a short swim and frolic for a mere $150 per person at **Hawk's Cay Resort**. Cute, young, swim suited beauties, billed as "marine biologists," frolic with you and the dol-

MILE MARKERS

The **Overseas Highway** is conveniently marked every mile by a **Mile Marker** that tells you the distance from MM 0 in Key West. Most businesses on the Overseas Highway use this system for their address. Thus, MM 72.5 OS is 72 and one half miles from Key West and is on the Ocean Side of the highway (the left-hand side heading toward Key West). BS means Bay Side or the right hand side of the highway as you are heading toward Key West. Street numbers usually reflect the nearby mile marker.

phins in a therapeutic dolphin encounter session, somehow arranged so that it is difficult for you to photograph your family with the dolphins yourself. It's fun and you can buy nice pics from their professional photographers afterwards for yet more $$.

The beauty of the water and sea life around the Keys is easy to appreciate by taking a short walk on any of the old abandoned bridges left over from the Flagler railroad. The bridges near **Indian Key** are particularly good for a nature

SIGHTS

DOLPHIN ABUSE?

You decide. Most serious researchers agree that if a facility is charging the public money to swim with dolphins they are not conducting legitimate research or providing legitimate "therapy." If the dolphins weren't in cages, they wouldn't hang around with us; they'd head for open water in a hurry. So would I.

stroll. Bring a hat and sunscreen.

There are not many **sandy beaches** in the Keys and the Upper Keys have less of them than the rest. The northern part of Key Largo has a few places you can park and walk along the spectacularly wild shoreline looking for weird flotsam and strange jetsam. There are some patches of sand, but no real beach. Still, this is great beachcombing territory, as storms and hurricanes tend to throw interesting junk up into the mangroves and scrub just past the high tide line. If you can handle the bugs, you could find old bottles and Japanese fishing floats. The beaches on **Old Rhodes Key** and **Elliot Key** to the north of Key Largo are even nicer, but are accessible only by boat. They are usually quite deserted.

The quaint old abandoned bridges, now splendid fishing piers, are the remains of the Florida East Coast Railway Key West Extension. This remarkable feat of engineering was built by railroad and hotel magnate **Henry Flagler**, who was a major figure in Florida's development. The railroad was completed in 1912 but,

after repeatedly being damaged by hurricanes, was abandoned in 1935.

Evening

Have dinner at **Whale Harbor Inn.** The enormous seafood buffet is world-famous. This is not just another steam table joint. They have shrimp, crab, squid, prime rib, and the entire usual buffet stuff, but top quality and a better selection than you usually see.

After your wonderful day in the Keys, drive back to Miami in the dark with a backseat full of sleeping kids and wet

ALTERNATE PLAN

An afternoon spent fishing is never wasted, even if you don't catch anything. But if you go with Captain Ron, you'll almost certainly have a **wahoo, amberjack, king** or **yellowtail** for dinner that night. Cap'n Ron has been putting guests on the fish for over 25 years. *Info: Captain Ron Green, Tel. 305-852-9577.*

bathing suits, and try not to have a head-on collision. Watch out for police roadblocks.

A WEEKEND IN THE UPPER KEYS

A full weekend in the Upper Keys gives you plenty of time to indulge in **water sports**— scuba diving/snorkeling, kayaking, fishing—and still have plenty of time left for poolside relaxation and consumption of seafood and tropical adult beverages. If you manage to avoid the worst of the traffic, you can get from downtown to Key Largo in a couple of hours. It's only 60 miles to Key Largo from the Miami airport.

Stock up on groceries, beer

and gas in Homestead. A few miles past Homestead and the end of the Florida Turnpike, the route to the Keys splits and you have a choice of staying on US 1 over **Jewfish Creek** to Key Largo, or take the route that goes through **Card Sound** to Key Largo so you can stop at **Alabama Jack's** for a few beers or rum concoctions and some crab cakes to get in the proper Keys mood. Alabama Jack's is a good introduction to the Keys, and is fairly typical of Keys drink emporiums. The

SIGHTS

Card Sound route involves a minor $1.50 toll and takes a little longer.

Careful! The speed limit on the Overseas Highway is, for the most part, 55 mph with a few areas of 45 mph and some school zones down to 30 mph. Radar traps are common. The road has long stretches with only two lanes, and there are few good places to pass. The highway is lined with small businesses, attractions, motels and other roadside urban stuff and there is a lot of local traffic. Hurrying on the Overseas Highway is rarely possible and never a good idea. On holiday weekends (Memorial Day, July 4th, etc), traffic is usually bumper-to-bumper from Homestead to Key West.

Friday Evening
Shortly after you hit Key Largo, check in at the wonderful **Kona Kai Resort** just opposite Ballyhoo's, or at **Casa Morada** a little further down the road. Both are upscale, quiet and small boutique hotels with wonderful frontage on the Gulf. Kona Kai has tennis. Casa Morada has bocce.

After checking in, you can stroll across the street from Kona Kai to **Ballyhoo's** for beer and wonderful seafood. A nice yellowtail or a Florida lobster tail is hard to beat and costs under $20.

If you still have some daylight left after dinner, drive on south a ways and take a stroll out on the bridges at MM 80 near **Indian Key** and **Lignum Vitae Keys**. The sea and bird life (such as cormorants and pelicans) you can see from these old abandoned railroad bridges is hard to believe. Tarpon, sharks and huge stingrays are easy to spot in the clear, shallow water.

The **Lorelei Cabana Bar** is the spot for enjoying tropical beverages and conch fritters while listening to island sounds. They almost always have some sort of live entertainment in the evenings. It can get crowded. Great!

SIGHTS

The **Caribbean Club** is supposedly the place where the movie *Key Largo* was filmed. Probably so. Their house band has been around for several decades and they are open late, late. Beer and the usual blender drinks are the deal. They just hose the place out every morning and start all over again.

Saturday
On Saturday morning, if your hotel doesn't throw you a nice breakfast, there is really little choice other than to hit the wonderful **Harriett's** for one of those enormous biscuits and gravy, grits, fried potatoes, eggs, coffee and all that kind of stuff breakfasts.

You might want to go ahead and get a sack lunch here for later in the day. Some of the fishing or diving boats expect you to bring your own lunch. Be prepared. Let Harriett do it for you.

With only one full day to indulge your Keys fantasy, you can make the most of it by doing a **two-tank dive** in the morning and **fishing the flats** in the afternoon. After all that time in the sun having fun drinking beer, we'll rely on a

seafood dinner and plenty of blender drinks to keep us going into the night.

The morning dive will be with **Dive In's** six pack (no more than six divers on the boat) trip to **John Pennekamp Coral Reef State Park**, where you can do a first dive at **Grecian Rocks** or **French Reef**. After that, perhaps the wreck of the **Benwood** or the **Bibb**. You should be back at your hotel in time for lunch.

If you are still full of energy after diving, a quick shower at the hotel should be followed by a long and beery lunch at **Pierre's at Morada Bay**. Be sure to try the seafood bisque. Delicious!

Without even taking time for a nap, head offshore with one of the fishing guides below for an afternoon trolling for the **man in the blue suit** (sailfish) or jigging up colossal

SIGHTS

amberjack. Fishing doesn't get any better than this.

There are dozens of fishing guides and charter boats as well as a couple of party boats in the area.

Several local restaurants, including **Ballyhoo's** and the **Fish House**, may be talked into preparing your catch for your dining pleasure. It's hard to beat eating fresh fish, drinking cold beer and telling lies about it all after a long day in the Keys.

On **Sunday**, take a short nature walk out on the bridges at MM 80 near **Indian Key** and **Lignum Vitae Keys**. Then head back to Miami with a pause on the way back for a

ALTERNATE PLAN

Lounge around the pool all day Saturday enjoying refreshing tropical beverages. A couple of half-hour snorkel excursions in the shallow water in front of the resort can be followed by more pool time. Venture out in the evening to gorge on seafood and enjoy the sounds at one of the local music venues like Lorelei.

nice seafood lunch at Ballyhoo's in Islamorada.

If you are fueling your day with beer and blender drinks, you should have plenty of energy to keep going after dining. There are only a few nightlife selections in the Upper Keys. The **Lorelei Cabana Bar** often has live music in the evenings. Sometimes it's great. They are almost always packed. Try the conch fritters. **Coconuts Lounge** has live music most evenings, and when the show's over there, it's just starting at the **Caribbean Club**. **Woody's** is famous for the lack of clothes worn by their professional dancers and for the famous house band **Big Dick and the Extenders**. (Zane Grey Lounge is for cigar-waving yuppie posers. It's fake old. Reminds me of Vegas. I'd rather go to bed than hang out there).

Sunday
Eat breakfast again at **Harriette's** or, for the Latin flavor, try **Denny's Latin Café**. The coffee is the best around for many miles. Starbucks is right next door but why go to a chain when you can sample wonderful, authentic café con leche?

SIGHTS

If you didn't manage to go fishing or diving yesterday, you need to do so today. On the other hand, there are several great areas for kayaking in the Upper Keys. I particularly enjoy renting a kayak from **Robbie's** for a couple of hours and paddling over the flats to historic **Indian Key** or **Lignum Vitae Key**. There's plenty of interesting sea life to be seen, including stingrays, leopard rays, hammerhead sharks and patrolling tarpon. The extensive schools of tarpon rolling around Robbie's will give most anglers the shakes.

When you're near coral, remember: look, but don't touch!

Never touch any coral, ever. In fact it's wise not to touch anything on the reef. Bright orange fire coral can cause a nasty burn, and there are sharp sea urchins and other little nasties awaiting unwary fingers.

But the pain that fire coral might cause to your little pinky is nothing compared to what you'll do to the coral. Touching coral tends to kill the little organisms. It's even worse with gloves, which is why some dive shops discourage wearing them.

For lunch, a grouper sandwich with a pitcher of beer at **Snapper's** is tropical heaven. Try their conch fritters.

Captain Chan's Gulfstream Party Boat is a fairly new party (fishing) boat that docks at the Ocean Bay Marina. They leave at 1:00 for half-day reef fishing trips. It's almost guaranteed you'll come back with a cooler full of filets. They clean the fish for you, ice them down and stick them in your cooler for the trip back to Miami.

Otherwise, spend the day strolling along the beach (such as it is) on the north part of Key Largo waiting until it's time for dinner at **Marker 88**. This is one of the best seafood places in the Keys—and I've

> ## ALTERNATE PLAN
> Head back early taking the Card Sound Road route so you can stop at **Alabama Jack's** in Key Largo for one last grouper sandwich and margarita. Try the fritters. *Info: Tel. 305-248-8741.*

SIGHTS

tried hundreds of them. It's a little bit fancier than most. Their chowder is wonderful. The service is outstanding. The wine list is prodigious.

Now settle into your rental car for the long drive back to Miami. Make sure someone sober is driving. And look out for speed traps.

A WEEK IN THE UPPER KEYS

If you have an entire week to spend enjoying the Upper Keys, you'll have time to indulge in a couple of your favorite activities almost to excess. The **reefs offshore** and **waters around the Keys** are what the big deal is all about.

The Keys themselves and the drive through the Keys are a spectacle of scenery but what's in the water is where it's at.

Drive from Miami and check in to one of the wonderful, quiet waterfront resorts. Spend most of your days out on the water: **dive**, **fish**, and **kayak** through the mangroves. In the evenings, indulge yourself shamelessly in **seafood** and **umbrella drink consumption**.

Day One
The Upper Keys are convenient to the Miami airport by car. If you manage to avoid most of the traffic, you can get

from downtown Miami to Key Largo in a couple of hours. It's only 60 miles to Key Largo from the Miami airport. See Chapter 10, *Practical Matters,* for the best route out of town. Remember, do the speed limit once you hit the Keys!

Just before you leave the mainland, there is a "Y" in the road and you are offered two routes to Key Largo.

The right hand choice, US 1, goes through an area of mangrove swamps and small lakes, over politically incorrectly named **Jewfish Creek**, and on to Key Largo. The road is being widened to four lanes and should make access to the Keys much faster early in 2010.

The left-hand route, Card Sound Road, goes through the same kind of swamps, past croc-filled **Lake Surprise**, past **Alabama Jack's** and through a modest tollbooth. This route

SIGHTS

takes about 15 minutes longer.

But wait! Back up and stop in for a beverage and a fish sandwich at funky **Alabama Jack's**. This is a real laid-back watering hole, very typical of the bars you will find further down the road. It's right in the swamp, so you should probably bring your mosquito repellant in with you from the car. Try the conch fritters. You'll love Jack's. If you don't, turn around and go to Disney World. You won't like the Keys.

Check into one of the upscale resorts like **The Moorings Village & Spa**, **Kona Kai** or the **Marriott Key Largo Beach Resort**. These are all nice. Kona Kai is small and quiet with tennis courts. The Moorings is a large resort on 18 acres. Beautiful. The Marriott is a very nice standard Marriott right on the bay, with all the usual amenities and water sports.

For dinner, get ready. You're going to drive right past **Ballyhoo's** in the center of the median. Their seafood is legendary, and they usually have an all-you-can-eat crab claw

deal for around $35. The beer is cold although the brand selection is mundane.

Snapper's, Bentley's Restaurant & Raw Bar, the Fish House, and the **Whale Harbor Inn** are good choices for seafood, seafood and seafood. Whale Harbor's seafood buffet is expensive but a great deal if you like to honk down huge piles of shrimp, crab, fish, etc. For a modest but great meal, try **Tower of Pizza**. Kids love it. The prices are honest and the food is good.

Days Two – Six
There is one absolutely great place for breakfast in the Upper Keys. **Harriett's** is one of those breakfast joints that have wonderful hot biscuits with all the usual down-home trimmings like gravy, grits, home fries, eggs, ham, sausage and toast. They'll do you up a nice sack lunch in case you need

SIGHTS

HURRICANES

Hurricane season officially lasts from June 1 to November 30 but hurricanes can come as late as December. From time to time tourists are asked to evacuate as approaching storms threaten and, rarely, everyone is asked to leave for the mainland. Monitor weather reports before and during your trip to the Keys during hurricane season. *Info: www.nhc.noaa.gov.*

one for a hike or trip on the water later in the day.

Anytime you have a couple of extra hours, especially in the evening after dinner but before dark, a walk on one of the abandoned **Flagler railroad bridges** is a wonderful idea. Not only do you get to see what the bridge fishermen are up to, but you can see a startling variety of sea life in the clear, shallow water as you stroll along. Sightings of stingrays, nurse sharks and horseshoe crabs are just about guaranteed. There are a couple of good bridges for this near Lower Matecumbe Key at MM 78.

Beachcombing and bird enthusiasts will enjoy walking on the ocean side beach at the north end of Key Largo. There is a small parking area. The rough beach goes on for a mile or two, but realize it is not a wonderful sandy beach like the ones you'll find from Miami north. This is an "interesting" beach with coral, seaweed and all sorts of washed up "junk" to examine.

Kayaking is particularly exciting in this same area.

The **John Pennekamp Coral Reef State Park** headquarters is worth a quick visit. I like to walk around the grounds for a look at the birds. There is a small swimming area. Keep in mind that by far the bulk of and the most interesting part of the park is offshore.

Coral reefs are what it is all about. You can arrange for snorkel, scuba or glass-bottomed

SIGHTS

boat trips to enjoy the spectacular reefs in and around the park. Dive operators throughout the Keys offer morning and afternoon dives. **Island Reef Divers** and **Dive In** offer two-tank dives in small boats.

Note: To boost tourism to the park, some years ago authorities decided to sink **a medium sized statue of Christ in the middle of a coral reef**. For reasons that are a puzzle to me, this statue is quite a draw, with divers coming from all over the world to see it. It's a medium-sized statue of Christ. Underwater. With all due respect, skip this lame excuse for a tourist attraction and spend your valuable time exploring the reefs.

Wreck diving is quite popular. Trips to the **Bibb, Duane, El Capitán**, and the **Spiegel Grove** are standouts. There are hundreds of reefs to choose from. Most of the usual ones are fairly busy with tourists. My favorites include some of the popular spots like **French Reef** and **Pickles Reef**, but I really like to get north of the park to some of the less-visited reefs like **Sassy's Bight, Pacific Reef** or **Carysfort**.

Hen & Chickens is a somewhat shallow dive with massive coral mounds. It makes a good spot for your second tank. The visibility is sometimes not as good as sites a little further out. A calm morning is the best time to visit.

There are several ways to enjoy **fishing** in the area. The easiest, and the most likely to end up with you catching fish, is to hire a guide for the day. Flats fishing for bonefish, tar-

SIGHTS

hat and sunscreen). **Bridge fishing** may seem a little down-market at first, but it's nothing to be ashamed of. It's fun, you might catch some fish, and you have an excuse to piddle around the bridges talking to old salts, fool around with your fishing tackle and poke at crabs.

There are dozens of fishing guides and charter boats as well as a couple of party boats in the area.

pon and permit is usually done in a small skiff with two guests and the guide poling the boat around the sand and turtle grass flats. Trolling offshore for billfish will more likely find you coming home with dorado (mahi) and wahoo for dinner but that's all right. Most of the charter boats will take four to six people.

If you want to enjoy fishing and don't want to spend hundreds of dollars on a charter, you can simply buy some shrimp and head to one of the abandoned Flagler railroad bridges and join the rest of the bridge fishing brigade. This is a nice way to spend a few hours out on the water (bring something to drink, a

A pleasant way to waste an hour or so before or after dinner is to stroll around the marina near the Holiday Inn where the authentic **African Queen** is tied up. Bogart and Hepburn made it their home in the excellent classic movie *African Queen*. They do rides. The boat from *On Golden Pond* is also, inexplicably, tied up here. **Coconuts** is nearby, so you can grab one of your favorite tropical beverages when you get tired of strolling around the marina. They have decent (and sometimes great) bands most evenings.

The Upper Keys are not noted for nightlife, with one dubious exception. **Woody's** is a strip club perhaps most famous for their house band: **Big Dick and the Extenders**. I suppose this is not to be missed.

For a more sedate evening's entertainment, I suggest a couple of drinks at **Lorelei Cabana Bar**. If you can squeeze into a seat by water, you can see the cooks throwing scraps out the back of the kitchen to feed the enormous tarpon, which also seem to come by in the evenings for the live entertainment.

Snapper's and the **Caribbean Club** have bands - Snapper's is a bit mellower. The **Rum Runners Tiki Bar** at Holiday Isle always seems to have an annoying band. The very worst sort of cigar smoking, chocotini-sipping blagging yuppies inhabit the **Zane Grey Lounge**. It's overpriced and plastic. I can't stand the place.

Last Day
On the way back to Miami, I suggest stopping at all of the holy spots once again, including **Denny's Latin Café** in Key Largo for a kick-ass cup of Cuban Coffee. Remember, there are long stretches of two-lane highway. Nighttime driving here can be monotonous, and therefore dangerous.

BEST SLEEPS & EATS

Although there are few true budget options in the area other than camping, there is **a good variety of lodging**. The Keys are noted for waterfront resorts catering to anglers, divers and nature lovers. Although not dirt cheap, there are a few nice, clean and interesting less expensive lodging choices as well. A few well maintained, mom and pop-style motels are left over from the fifties, and make a good budget vacation choice.

The **selection of restaurants is great**, with something for everyone. Funky Cuban cafés compete with fancy-shmancy drizzly-sauce fusion places serving seafood with the very latest of west coast/Pac Rim/mojo sauce-smothered grouper cheeks. Or whatever. There are a couple of wonderful hole-in-the-wall joints where steaming hot fresh seafood comes to you on waxed paper. Delicious!

SIGHTS

SLEEPS & EATS

SLEEPS & EATS

KEY LARGO
Amy Slate's Amoray Dive Center & Resort $$$

If you are more interested in diving than anything else, and don't fancy the chain hotels, Amoray is a good choice. It's a privately owned dive resort, and their main focus is on diving and instructional vacations. The dive operation is professional.

The lodgings are comfortable and close to the boat dock so you can simply step off the boat at the end of your dive, walk a few steps to your room and hop in the shower. It's clean and neat and some rooms have kitchens. There is a nice pool and the water-front has areas to lie about enjoying beverages. Prices are a little better than in more built-up areas of the Keys. *Info: MM 104.2 BS, Key Largo. www.amoray.com; Tel. 305-451-3595.*

Bay Cove Motel $$

Bay Cove is small, friendly and comfortable, with an island feel. There is a bit of sand on the waterfront. They have a great dock for hanging out, and are located close to several dive operators. It's a good budget choice. *Info: MM 99.4 BS, Key Largo. www.baycovemotel.com; Tel. 305-451-1686.*

Hilton Key Largo Resort $$$$

Once a Westin, once a Sheraton, the Grande is now a Hilton.

After a $12 million refurbishment, the place shines. There is a wonderful view from the upper floors look-ing out over the gulf—be sure you insist on

BEST OF THE BEST IN THE UPPER KEYS

Kona Kai Resort $$$$

Convenient to Miami, good restaurants, the ocean side reefs and the bayside flats, Kona Kai is also a quiet oasis—no kids, no phones, no problems. There is a nice dock, pool, and lighted tennis courts. They even have a small wading beach. Manatees frequent the wading beach area. The wonderful Ballyhoo's is right across the street. The rooms are all unique, large, well-appointed with CDs, DVDs, kitchen facilities. *Distinctive Luxury Hotels of the World* lists Kona Kai. Always a sign of a well-managed property, the owners, Joe and Veronica Harris, live on the property. *Info: MM 97.8 BS, Key Largo. www.konakairesort.com; Tel. 305-852-7200, 800-365-7829.*

a room with a sea view. As the name implies, the Grande is big (200 rooms), and has little of the lovely Keys flavor found in smaller, more intimate hotels in the area. They do have just about everything you could want on a vacation under one roof. The main restaurant serves up fine seafood. It's generally expensive, which to me means you're not necessarily getting good value. Bar drinks can run over $10 each, and the bar is not twice as nice as others in the area. *Info: MM 97 BS, Key Largo. www.keylargoresort.com; Tel. 888-871-3437, 305-852-5553.*

Alabama Jack's $$

Jack's really is the last place to buy a drink before you get to the Keys. The bridge to Key Largo is right next to the place. Cold beer, fish sandwiches, and cold beer are on the menu. The food is great and the atmosphere is very much in the Keys mold. There are no windows or much in the way of doors, and it's located right on the edge of a large mangrove swamp, so bring your mosquito repellent inside with you. Drinks are served in authentic Keys

SLEEPS & EATS

BEST OF THE BEST RESTAURANTS IN THE UPPER KEYS
Ballyhoo's $$$

This is one of my very favorite restaurants in the Keys. It's not at all fancy, and not particularly cheap, but they move a lot of sea-

food through the place—this is the real deal. Conch chowder is a favorite. Ask about any particular daily specials. I find it hard to pass up yellowtail. They offer it Française, Nassau baked, meunière, fried, picatta, broiled, or stuffed with real crab. However, the best thing about Ballyhoo's is the all-you-can-eat special. Stone crab claws are usually the deal, for around $35 or so. You don't have to make a pig of yourself. Heavy eaters can honk down 25 or 30 claws. A couple of serious fatties reportedly did a few over 60 each. Ouch! They have a small but decent wine list and a good selection of beer. Of course they also have steaks, chicken, salads and burgers. Don't miss this one. *Info: MM 97.8, in the Median, Key Largo. www.ballyhoosrestaurant.com; Tel. 305-852-0822.*

style—in a plastic cup. I like Jack's, and almost always take the slightly longer route to Key Largo that goes past it. It's just a funky swamp-side bar, but it is typical of the places further down the road you will likely be patronizing so check it out. If you don't like Jack's, you should probably get back in the car, turn around and head north to Disney World—you won't like the rest of the Keys either. *Info: Card Sound Road, Key Largo. Tel. 305-248-8741.*

Anthony's Italian Restaurant $$
With a few exceptions, most of the tables in Anthony's are kind of dark, but Anthony's has all the usual Italian specialties you love, plus fresh seafood and steaks. The calzones are good and they have a proper lounge. *Info: MM 97.6 in the median, Key Largo. Tel. 305-853-1177.*

Denny's Latin Café $

Located in a small shopping center right next to Starbuck's, Denny's has no relation to the vapid chain of the same name. It's a *muy auténtico* Cuban restaurant with wonderful coffee and great, stick-to-your-ribs stews, soups and island specials. Typical Cuban dinners such as roast chicken or pork come spread across three plates, at

unbelievably low prices. You can get small shots of inky Cuban espresso for a mere 80¢. Two of these and you'll be flying. You can sit on a little bench outside under a tree and enjoy your cup with a couple of ancient locals. *Info: MM 100, BS, Key Largo. Tel. 305-451-3665.*

Fish House $$$

Fresh seafood done up conch style is supposed to be the deal here, and they do deliver. They

KEYS DINING

You can get excellent seafood in the Keys if you know where to go (which you will as soon as you've finished reading this book). However, there are hundreds of mediocre (or worse) restaurants tempting tourists with plastic décor and overpriced frozen seafood that has nothing to do with Florida. Look for a funky place with local license plates in the parking lot, and stick with local specialties like yellowtail.

Conch and lobster are local favorites. The large "Key West" shrimp should be fresh and local (smaller generic "shrimp" may come from farms in Central America or Vietnam). **Yellowtail snapper** is an excellent local fish ("red snapper" is not red, definitely not local, and probably not even snapper). A wonderful local staple is the fish formerly known as dolphin. In order to avoid confusion with the marine mammal of the same name, *coryphaena hippurus* (a delicious, firm white fish) is now generally referred to as **mahi mahi** (or dorado).

have a large assortment of local fish on the menu, including some you don't see everywhere, such as cobia and black grouper. Try

SLEEPS & EATS

the conch fritters. The adjacent Fish House Encore is a slightly more upscale and inventive version of pretty much the same menu items. Encore has a modest wine list. *Info: MM 102.4 OS, Key Largo. www.fishhouse.com; Tel. 305-451-HOOK.*

Harriette's $

Harriette's is a good ol' fashion place to get a stonking great breakfast with biscuits and gravy, grits, home fries, eggs over easy and all the trimmings. They have hearty lunch specials and will pack a box lunch for you. You can call ahead or have them do up the lunch while you scarf breakfast. *Info: MM 95.7 BS, Key Largo. Tel. 305-852-8689.*

ISLAMADORA & DUCK CAY

Caloosa Cove Resort $$$

On the ocean with a marina and all the expected resort goodies, the slightly upscale Caloosa is all suites and efficiencies. There is a grocery store and restaurant, so you could stay right here and do your whole holiday thing without even having to walk very far. The pool is nice and the bar is busy. This is a good choice for travelers who don't want to have to go anywhere much outside the resort, but want to be able to take part in diving, fishing and other Keys activities. *Info: MM 73.8 OS, Islamorada. www.caloosacove.com; Tel. 305-664-8856.*

Casa Morada $$$$

The very upscale Casa Morada is a wonderfully renovated old motel done up in high Miami Beach style. It's very well done. The rooms are a little on the small side, but they are luxuriously appointed. Everyone raves about the good service. The staff is young, trendy and attentive. Rooms have small refrigerators stocked with complimentary fruit juice, water and other delectables. The grounds are private, with interesting plantings. There is a small "island" in back by the bay with a place to lounge around and enjoy the view out over the flats to Everglades National Park. The tiki bar is very nicely situated near the water so you can watch manatees and dolphins cavort about. They have bocce. Trendy! The complimentary breakfast is great. You're unlikely to need to buy breakfast out unless you simply must have a grease fix. A variety of coffees, and a little bit more than the usual B&B breakfast goodies are generously laid out along with newspapers from around the world. What a great way to start the day! *Info: MM 82 BS, Islamorada. www.casamorada.com; Tel. 305-664-0044.*

Cheeca Lodge $$$$

Cheeca has the resort amenities most vacationers want. It is nicely landscaped, and built around a smallish golf course. There

is lots of green. It's a fairly large resort, and the nice pool and other public areas are usually pretty well packed with teenagers and kids. The restaurant has reasonably good (if overpriced) food but the service, like much of the service I encountered at Cheeca, is slow and not particularly sharp. The waterfront is not very attractive, but the same could be said of most waterfronts in the Keys. They have a long dock, which is nice for an evening stroll. The beachside bungalows are by far the nicest rooms. Cheeca is making an effort to sell itself as an up market property, but they are not quite there. It's a pretty nice four-star type of resort, but I never felt comfortable here. I prefer a smaller, more laid-back, friendlier atmosphere. *Info: MM 82 OS, Islamorada. www.cheeca.com; Tel. 305-664- 4651.*

Chesapeake Resort $$$

Getting a little long in the tooth and in need of renovation, the Chesapeake is certainly a decent option, but don't expect to be wowed. The property is nice, but there is really no beach to speak of. Some of the rooms are on the noisy side as one end of the building is near the highway. Located right next to the wonderful Whale Harbor Inn restaurant, the Chesapeake is also convenient to the charter fishing docks. They offer all the usual diving and fishing trips. Check your bill carefully when you check out. Ask about any "resort fees" when you check in. *Info: MM 83.4 OS, Islamorada. www.chesapeake-resort.com; Tel. 305-664-4662.*

Days Inn Suites $$$

Much nicer than the usual interstate highway cloverleaf Days Inn, this is a high-rise building on the beach, such as it is. The rooms are clean, and some are quite large, with separate kitchens and bedrooms. Water sports rentals and marina pretty much sum up the "resort" amenities. It's a good base that's close to a couple of good restaurants. *Info: MM 82.7 OS, Islamorada. Tel. 305-664-3681.*

Hawk's Cay Resort $$$–$$$$

Hawk's Cay is a huge, busy resort, with all the goodies including dolphin interaction. The rooms in the main buildings are nothing

to get too excited about but the condo rentals are great (but pricey). Canal-side condo rentals come with everything, everything, everything you'll need for a Keys holiday. They are new and very nicely appointed. The older hotel rooms are beginning to show wear. The restaurants and snack areas are full of tourist cattle most of the time. The controversial and unconventional owner, Pritam Singh, is the largest real estate developer in the Keys, and this was one of his first developments. It's on the mass tourism end of things, and the service is rather impersonal. A large cage where dolphins are kept captive in the name of "dolphin encounters" dominates the beachfront area. *Info: MM 61 OS, Duck Key. www.hawkscay.com; Tel. 305-742-7000.*

Atlantic's Edge $$$$

Sadly, service and food have declined sharply at this formerly top-notch restaurant. Interesting seafood/tropical/Asian fusion things litter the menu, but quality and quantity were poor on my last visit, as was the service. Most of the reports I've gotten from fellow travelers say the same. *Info: MM 82 OS, Islamorada, in the Cheeca Lodge. Tel. 305-664-4651.*

The Islamorada Fish Company $$$

The IFC, their seafood market and the Zane Grey Lounge are both in the same complex as the Worldwide Sportsman/Bass Pro shopping mart. The restaurant has good food and a nice view. You can throw scraps into the water and watch tarpon gobble them up in a frenzy. The seafood seems quite fresh but the atmosphere is a bit plastic. You get a feeling of being just one more tourist sheep in line to be shorn. There are funkier places just down the road. *Info: MM 81.5 BS, Islamorada. Tel. 305-664-9271.*

Lorelei Cabana Bar Restaurant $$$

This is a great place to watch the sunset (or your fellow tourists) and listen to live music. The food is standard bar food, and most people like the atmosphere, which is quite casual. This is one of the few spots in the area to catch live music and sometimes the bands are quite good. *Info: MM 82, Islamorada. www.loreleicabanabar.com; Tel. 305-664-4656.*

Marker 88 Restaurant $$$

Reports I hear are spotty. Some say the food and service is great but others tell me the food is basic, the service slow and the prices high. When I visited I had a wonderful meal in all ways. There was an interesting selection of local seafood specialties and a decent wine list. I found the service to be fine. *Info: MM 88 BS, Islamorada. www.marker88.com; Tel. 305-852-9315.*

Pierre's at Morada Bay $$$$

Everyone says good things about Pierre's. The sunset view is great from the upstairs dining room. The downstairs Green Flash Lounge is elegant and tropical at the same time. I love their

SLEEPS & EATS

rosemary bread. Although a bit pricier than the other restaurants in the area, it's worth it (this means $35 for an entrée). Service and food are great. Of course, local seafood tops the menu. They have a nice selection of wines by the glass and a great selection by the bottle. Dinner only. *Info: MM 81.6 BS, Islamorada. Tel. 305-664-3225.*

Whale Harbor Inn $$$

The Whale Harbor has been a landmark since I was a little kid. On weekend trips down from Miami with my folks, we would

almost always stop for the huge seafood buffet on the way back. The food is waaay better than your average all-you-can-eat buffet. They have crab legs, shrimp and all the usual meats, veggies and salads you would expect. It's not cheap but you do get to eat piles of your favorite seafood. There's a conveniently placed slimming mirror in the lobby so you can check yourself out on the way out. You can leave thinner than when you came in—even if you did have three desserts! *Info: MM 83.9 OS, Islamorada. www.whaleharborrestaurant.com; Tel. 305-664-4959.*

BEST SHOPPING

There are a few places in the Upper Keys for souvenir shopping, with only a few old-style shell stores scattered among places to buy cheesy T-shirts. These are meager shopping opportunities, but there is one notable exception.

Worldwide Sportsman

This is a big store with a wonderful selection of fishing tackle. It's a great place to browse and stock up on the essentials and the exotic. They also have probably the best selection of T-shirts, Tommy Bahama and other resort-type clothes. The selection is good but the prices are at the top end of the scale. *Info: Islamorada, MM 81.5 BS.*

Shell World

You can't miss Shell World.

Both locations ooze big-time tourist shell store vibe. You can buy all the usual alligator items made from every material imaginable (including alligator), jewelry, Keys novelties, island wear and, of course, lots and lots of shells. They've got them by the bin. It's worth a short browse. *Info: MM 106 and 97.5.*

Hooked On Books
This is really your best choice for a bookstore in the Upper Keys. They have a decent selection and it is not one of the big chains so they are likely to have something a little different. *Info: MM 82.6 OS, Islamorada. Tel. 305-517-2602.*

BEST NIGHTLIFE & ENTERTAINMENT

The Upper Keys are not a mecca for nightlife. Coconuts and a couple of other places host live bands. There are a couple of late night bars catering primarily to locals working in the tourism business, and one comparatively tasteful strip club. Nearby Marathon boasts the wonderful Hurricane where you can enjoy live blues most nights.

Caribbean Club
The Caribbean Club is supposedly the place where the movie Key Largo was filmed. Probably so. Their house band has been around for several decades and they are open late, late (back in the old days, before DUI laws were enforced, the place was open 24 hours, and had no doors). Beer and the usual blender drinks are the deal. They hose the place out every morning and start all over again. *Info: MM 104 BS, Key Largo. Tel. 305-451-4466.*

Coconuts Lounge
Coconuts is at the edge of an upscale marina, so you can stroll around the marina gawking at boats when you get tired of guzzling your favorite tropical beverages. They have single strummers on the deck most every day, and bands inside on weekends. *Info: MM 100 OS, Key Largo in the Marina del Mar Resort. Tel. 305-453-9794.*

Rum Runners
A collection of thatched, elevated tiki huts makes up

SHOPPING NIGHTLIFE & ENTERTAINMENT

the more or less open-air bar. The bar is famous for the namesake drink created there by Holiday Isle proprietor Joe Roth. This involved careful, lengthy research. They have live bands some nights. Call for details. The crowd seems to get younger as the night gets older. *Info: At Holiday Isle Resort marina, MM 84 OS, Islamorada. Tel. 305-664-2321.*

Lorelei Cabana
A great place to enjoy the sunset, do some people-watching, and listen to live music (*photo below*). The slightly fancy bar food is okay, and most people like the casual atmosphere. One of the few spots in the area to catch live music – sometimes it's quite good. *Info: MM 82, Islamorada. Tel. 305-664-4656.*

Snappers
Happy hour is the main reason to go to Snappers. It's on the water with a nice view, but it's not a sunset watching spot. Locals pack the place when the live bands start. Call ahead for the schedule. The food is okay but expensive, and the service can be poor (see *Best Eats*). *Info: MM 94.5 OS, Key Largo. Tel. 305-852-5956.*

Woody's Saloon & Restaurant
The famous adult entertainment venue Woody's continues in the grand tradition. Notorious band Big Dick & the Extenders provide raucous music and adult comedy. Happy hour is 4pm-8pm and they are open until 4am. *Info: MM 82 BS, Islamorada. Tel. 305-664-4335.*

BEST SPORTS & RECREATION

DIVING & SNORKELING

You don't need any excuse to get out on the water and marvel at the splendor of the **coral reefs**. If you visit the Keys and never get to **snorkel, dive or fish** in the waters around the islands, you have missed one of the very best things about the Keys.

Snorkeling and scuba diving conditions in the Keys are the best in the US. There are miles of reefs with drop-offs, caves, sandy channels and all manner of exotic reef fish. The edge of the **Gulf Stream** is immediately adjacent to the reefs, bringing pelagic creatures close in for your viewing (and fishing) pleasure.

Snorkeling and scuba diving are easy to do and there are many shops in the area ready to teach visitors so they can enjoy the **spectacular reefs**.

From well north of Miami to well west of Fort Jefferson, a chain of coral reefs protects the Keys from ocean swells rolling in from Africa (coral experts call this a fringing reef system). The reefs harbor millions of animal species, from fish to crustaceans to mollusks to sponges and sea squirts. Teeming reef life is one of the cornerstones of the world ecology and the reefs of the Keys are a living, breathing reason to become aware of and practice sustainable lifestyles. The reefs are easy to get to, and they won't be around forever, so you owe it to yourself (and especially to your kids) to get out there and see them firsthand.

Never touch any coral, ever. In fact it's wise not to touch anything out on the reef. Bright orange fire coral can cause a nasty burn, and there are sharp sea urchins and other nasties awaiting unwary fingers. But the pain that fire coral might cause to your little pinky is nothing compared to what you'll do to the coral. Touching coral tends to kill the little organisms. It's even worse with gloves, which is why some dive shops discourage wearing them.

Be sure you select a scuba or snorkel trip that suits you. If you have never snorkeled before, be sure to ask for a beginner's trip so they don't

SPORTS & RECREATION

throw you over the side in 80 feet of water with a bunch of gung-ho scuba divers. If you are a hardcore Diver Dan type, try to be sure you don't end up spending the day on patch reefs in 10 feet of water when you would rather be exploring below deck on the wreck of the **Benwood**. Call or visit the dive operators and ask about specific trips that match your skill level.

You can arrange for snorkel, scuba or glass bottomed boat trips to enjoy the spectacular reefs. Dive operators throughout the Keys offer morning and afternoon dives. **Island Reef Diver** and **Dive In** offer two-tank dives in small boats.

Of course, the best-known diving area in the Upper Keys is **John Pennekamp Coral Reef State Park**. There are dozens of wonderful dive and snorkel sites to choose from.

Skip the twee underwater **Christ of the Deep** statue. You can see a similar statue on dry land for free. The huge park area has protected the reefs and, as a result, the coral and fish life is more intense here than in most other parts of the Keys.

The **John Pennekamp Coral Reef State Park** headquarters is worth a quick visit. I like to walk around the grounds for a look at the birds. There is a small swimming area. Keep in mind that by far largest and most interesting part of the park is offshore. The **glass bottom boat** *Spirit of Pennekamp* leaves twice daily from the marina at park headquarters. They also rent boats and kayaks.

There are hundreds of reefs to choose from. Most of the close-in ones are fairly busy with cattle boats. My favorites include some of the popular spots such as **French Reef** and **Pickles Reef**, but I really like to get north of the park to some of the less-visited reefs like **Sassy's Bight**, **Pacific Reef**, or Carysfort.

Other popular dive sites include shallow patch reefs like

Hen and Chickens. Hen and Chickens is a somewhat shallow dive with massive coral mounds. It makes a good second-tank spot. The visibility is sometimes not as good as sites a little further out. A calm morning is a good time for a visit. **Molasses, French** and **Pickles Reefs** are famous dive choices a little further out along the edge of the Gulf Stream.

Hard-core Diver Dan types will love the huge wrecks just outside the park boundaries. The *Spiegel Grove, Benwood, Bibb, USS Alligator* and several others make for weeks of wreck diving if that's what gets you going.

Excellent patch reefs, wrecks and rarely-visited Gulf Stream edge reefs lure the more adventurous to the areas to the north of Key Largo. This area is harder to reach, as there are no roads or marina facilities on the keys to the north of Key Largo. Reefs extend all the way up to Miami and most see few visitors. Dive sites like **Sassy's Bight** are secrets that local divers try to keep to themselves. Most dive operators claim they have not heard of some of the more interest-

ing sites to the north. It takes more gas to get to them. They may just want to save them for themselves.

Amoray Dive Center
Amy Slate probably offers the most comfortable diving in the Keys. They combine a complete diving and training center with comfortable lodging all in a quiet, shaded compound. You have only a few feet to walk from your room to the dive boat. Luxury! They have a large catamaran for groups and a smaller boat for custom 6-pack dives. *Info: MM 104.2 BS, Key Largo. www.amoray.com; Tel. 305-451-3595.*

Dive In
Specializing in custom dive trips, Dive In runs only boats with six or fewer divers per trip. This is good. You're more likely to be able to select dive sites appropriate to your skill level and interest with smaller

SPORTS & RECREATION

CORAL REEFS

Coral is a communal organism. The colorful formations you see are colonies of thousands of tiny animals, which filter food from the water. The calcium they secrete builds a coral reef over hundreds of years. The coral attracts tiny fish and crustaceans, which attract larger predators, and so up the scale. A living reef is an **incredibly complex ecosystem,** which provides habitat for many important fish species. Like rain forests, reefs worldwide are slowly disappearing. Pollution, sedimentation and overfishing chip away at the reefs. Whatever the future holds, The Keys' reefs are beautiful now, so get out and enjoy them!

dive groups. They are on the ocean side, so the runs to the reefs are short. They are a PADI operation and offer all the usual instructions and certifications. *Info: MM 97.5 OS, Key Largo. www.diveinflkeys.com; Tel. 305-852-1919.*

Island Reef Diver
Island Reef runs boats with eight or fewer divers and offers NAUI instruction. They are a full-service dive shop. *Info: 3 Seagate Blvd., Key Largo (turn at MM 100 OS). Tel. 305-453-9456.*

Quiescence Diving Services
These guys run three boats, each with a maximum of six divers. They will personalize your trip if you are chartering the whole boat. Early morning, half-day, all day, night dives, whatever. Their instruction is both NAUI and PADI certified. Check in advance for a fuel surcharge so you won't be surprised on the day of your dive. *Info: MM 103.5. www.keylargodiving.com; Tel. 305-451-2440.*

Ocean Quest Dive Center
Located behind Smuggler's Cove Resort, Ocean Quest runs medium-sized boats with a maximum of 12 divers each.

Their instruction covers both NAUI and PADI. They will try to be flexible with dive sites but if you have specific requests such as wreck dives, you may need to try to schedule a day or two in advance. *Info: MM 88.5, Islamorada. www.oceanquest divecenter.com; Tel. 305-664-4401.*

FISHING

The Keys are one of North America's top fishing destinations, with three main types of angling action. **Bonefish, permit, tarpon** (*photo at right*) and other exotics school up around the flats and channels. **Huge snapper, grouper, yellowtail** and **kingfish** swarm around the reefs. **Marlin, amberjack, sails, snook, trout, bonefish,** and **dorado** lurk just offshore in the Gulf Stream. The best tarpon months are April, May, and June. The bonefish are in the area year-round but the best months are in the spring and fall.

Several "humps" rise from the floor of the **Gulf Stream,** causing current upwellings that concentrate baitfish and attract game fish. Savvy charter captains punch the GPS coor-

dinates of these humps into their autopilots and help guests hook up billfish, tuna or wahoo.

There are several ways to enjoy fishing in the Keys. The easiest, and the most likely to end up with you catching fish, is to charter a boat for the day. Flats fishing for bonefish, tarpon and permit is usually done in a small skiff with two guests and the guide poling the boat around the sand and turtle grass flats. Trolling offshore for billfish will more likely find you coming home with dorado (mahi) and wahoo for dinner, but that's all right.

If you want to enjoy fishing and don't want to spend hundreds of dollars on a charter, you can simply buy some shrimp and head to one of the abandoned Flagler railroad bridges and join the rest of the bridge fishing brigade. This is a nice way to spend a

SPORTS & RECREATION

SPORTS & RECREATION

few hours (bring something to drink, a hat and sunscreen) out on the water. **Bridge fishing** may seem a little downmarket at first, but it is nothing to be ashamed of. It's fun, you might catch some fish, and you have an excuse to piddle around the old bridges talking to old salts, fool around with your fishing tackle and poke at crabs.

The best time to fish the Keys is whenever you happen to be there. However, you can expect the best action from November through March to be for sailfish, tuna, amberjack, shark, kingfish, snapper and grouper. April through October is usually best for dolphin, tuna, wahoo, yellowtail, grouper, snapper and shark.

Captain Bob Jones

Captain Bob is primarily a flats guide specializing in fly-fishing for bonefish, and permit. He also likes to fish live mullet and large crabs on circle hooks for tarpon. The hookup rate is much better with circle hooks, and it is much easier to release the fish unharmed after the battle. A half-day runs $350 and all day is $450. Captain Bob offers a unique night fly-

fishing tarpon trip for $350. What a great trip! Imagine battling tarpon at night! They are a very difficult fish to tame even in the daytime. "You would be surprised how aggressively they eat a fly at night." *Info: Islamorada. www.jonesfishing.com; Tel. 305-517-2953.*

Captain Ron Green

My family has been fishing with Captain Ron for three decades and he has always absolutely busted his hump to find us memorable fish. He's fun to be with, but serious about his business: putting his clients on the fish. The Daytripper III is fast and comfortable, equipped with the latest fish finding electronics and a captain who knows how to use them. Ask him to take you jigging on "The Hump." *Info: Tavernier. www.daytrippercharters.com; Tel. 305-852-9577.*

Captain Chan's Gulfstream Party Boat

A party boat (some call it a head boat) is a cheaper alternative to a charter. It's a large boat that makes regular trips, charging on a per-person basis. Captain Chan's offers day and night fishing trips from

$45. You just bring your drinks and food. They leave from the docks at Ocean Bay Marina. *Info: MM 99.5, Key Largo. Tel. 305-451-9788.*

Miss Islamorada

Another local party boat is Miss Islamorada, which leaves every day at 9:30am from Bud N' Mary's Marina for daylong trips. For a mere $60 they supply everything but food and drinks. The crew helps with bait and fish handling. Your catch will be neatly filleted and handed to you iced down in a handy filet bag at the end of the day. *Info: MM 79.8 OS, Islamorada, Bud N' Mary's. www.miss-islamadora.com; Tel. 800-742-7945.*

BOATING

Renting a car while on vacation in an unfamiliar area is a great way to see the sights around you. Renting a boat in the Keys is much the same (as long as you know what you're doing). The best things about the Keys are in the water and you need a boat to get to them.

There is a wide variety of boat rental operators. Check their web sites and call in advance to be sure they have the type of boat and equipment you need. Be sure to reserve well in advance. Some rental operators will deliver the boat if you are renting for several days.

John Pennekamp Coral Reef State Park

You can rent boats at park headquarters at the marina. The boats are fairly basic 18- to 23-foot center consoles with Bimini tops, quite good enough for fishing, diving or just noodling around. Prices range up to $350 per day for the largest, a 23-footer. You must reserve in advance. *Info: Key Largo, MM 102.5 OS. www.pennekamppark.com; Tel. 305-451-6325.*

Bump and Jump

All their fishing boats come with GPS, fish finders, live wells and other necessary goodies. Divers are catered to as well. Many of their boats

SPORTS & RECREATION

are big enough to take off-shore. They also have a variety of flats skiffs available. They deliver all over the Keys for longer rentals. *Info: Key Largo, MM 99.7. Islamorada, MM 74.5. Tel 305-664-9494.*

Robbie's Boat Rentals
Robbie's is basically a marina where you can rent small boats and kayaks. They also organize trips to nearby **Indian Key** and **Lignumvitae Key**. It's at the base of a bridge near the tiny (10 acres) **Indian Key State Park** and other interesting places to explore. But the big deal at Robbie's is the hundreds of wild tarpon that congregate around the dock waiting for handouts of fish scraps tossed in by tourists. Robbie's sells buckets of nasty fish scraps so you can go out on the dock and get the tarpon going. They put on quite a show thrashing around in the water fighting over fish guts. It's a rare chance to observe the **Silver King** up close. Kids love it. *Info: MM 77.5 BS. Tel. 305-664-9814.*

Houseboat Vacations of the Florida Keys
These large, comfortable houseboats can sleep up to 8 people in relative comfort.

They have several models, and also rent kayaks, skiffs and all sorts of other watercraft to add to your fun. These boats need to be kept in Florida Bay only—they are not the type of boat that you can take out scuba diving on the reefs or trolling in the Gulf Stream. *Info: Islamorada, MM 86. www.thefloridakeys.com/houseboats; Tel. 305-664-4009.*

Boating in the Keys is not quite like driving. There are no street signs or stop signs. Most of the water around the Keys is very shallow, and sand bars and reefs pop up unexpectedly. Damage to props on rental boats is routine. There are extremely stiff fines for damaging coral or sand and grass flats with your boat or its propeller. The fines are calculated by the square inch of damage to the bottom of the sea. Damage to the bottom of your boat is a matter between you and the rental operator. Unless you know what you're doing, do your boating with guides, in their boats.

ATTRACTIONS
It is remarkable and refreshing to note how few cheesy

roadside attractions there are in the Keys, compared to more developed regions of Florida. The natural splendor of the area remains the main attraction. There are a couple of **dolphin-experience** operations and the famous **Theater of the Sea**. Not much else.

African Queen
It's true, this is the boat that was used to make the movie with Humphrey Bogart and Katherine Hepburn. The movie had nothing to do with Florida or Key Largo, but the whole *Key Largo* movie thing seems to mean that this is a good place for anything Bogartish. Kind of like Hemingway stuff in Key West. Rides are $15 per person. The launch used in *On Golden Pond* is also nearby for gawking. *Info: Key Largo at the Holiday Inn, MM 100. Tel. 305-451-4655.*

Theater of the Sea
Features the usual porpoise and sea lion shows. The park bills itself as a **Marine Mammal Adventure Park** (whatever that is). They offer ecotours, dolphin swims, sea lion swims, stingray swims and other "exciting" eco-programs. Kids love it, and I suppose they might learn something valuable. If you want to swim with the confined dolphins, reserve in advance and get your checkbook ready. *Info: MM 84.7 OS. www.theaterofthesea.com; Tel. 305-664-2431.*

Dolphins Plus
Swim with the dolphins? If you have two kids and let them do the whole schmear, expect to pay in excess of $600 for the fun. Be careful of promises - you only get a few minutes actually in the water with a dolphin. Getting ready, orientation, and lectures take up the rest of the time. As with most of these operations, you cannot position yourself to get decent pictures of your kids having fun. The house photographer has complete access, and gets good full frontal pictures, which you can buy for a mere $60. "Cash in on the dolphins" is a more accurate description of this

SPORTS & RECREATION

operation. *Info: Key Largo. www.dolphinsplus.com; Tel. 866-860-7946.*

Florida Keys Wild Bird Rehabilitation Center

This is a far more worthy wild-life attraction, a center where Upper Keys volunteers take in injured, lost or stolen birds, nurse them back to health and set them free to resume their little birdy lives. The goal is to reduce the suffering of injured birds and reduce the causes of their injuries. Fine goals. This is a wonderful opportunity to see wild birds up close. It's a dream for photographers. Tours of the facilities must be arranged in advance. *Info: Tavernier, MM 93.6 OS. www.fkwbc.org; Tel. 305-852-4486.*

GOLF

The small and crowded Keys are definitely not golf territory, although there are several fine courses just to the north around Miami. One resort, **Cheeca Lodge**, has a small but smart Jack Nicklaus designed nine-holer. Non-guests can call for reservations. *Info: Islamorada. Tel. 305-664-4651.*

BIRDING

All the Keys are known for their spectacular birding possibilities. The Upper Keys in particular are a good area for shore birds and transients. **Warblers** are the stars of the show. Look for palm, Cape May, worm-eating, prairie, black-throated blue, blackpoll and northern parula warblers, as well as white-eyed vireos. You should also be on the lookout for white-crowned pigeons, spotted sandpipers, indigo and painted buntings, bobolinks and gray kingbirds.

Look for **ospreys** nesting along the road, especially as you approach Key Largo from the mainland. Among the raptor family you should spot common and red-shouldered hawks.

Dagny Johnson Key Largo Hammock Botanical State Park

The park is an area of dry hardwood woodland where you can expect to see Cape May warblers, prairie warblers, four whiteeyed vireos, and thousands of LBBs (little brown birds). *Info: Open 8am-5pm. Key Largo. Tel. 305-451-1202.*

Birders will love the **Florida Keys Wild Bird Rehabilitation Center** (see previous page).

BEACHES, PARKS & ECO-WALKS

You can easily appreciate the beauty of the water and sea life around the Keys by taking a short walk on any of the old abandoned bridges left over from Flagler's abandoned railroad. The bridges near **Long Key** are particularly good for a nature stroll. Bring a hat and sunscreen.

Harry Harris Park & Beach

This is a small park with all the family recreational goodies. There is a diminutive protected swimming area. *Info: Tavernier, MM 93.5 OS.*

Annie's Beach

Annie's is a small but attractive park by the side of the road in Islamorada. There is a covered picnic area and a nice walk along a bit of sand. It's usually rather crowded but, if you don't see many cars as you pass by, stop for an enjoyable half-hour or so. *Info: MM 73.5 OS.*

KAYAKING

The shallow, calm water with channels meandering through mangroves and turtle grass flats makes the Keys perfect kayaking territory. There are hundreds of sites where you can easily plop in a couple of kayaks and, moments later, find yourself deep in the wilderness. **Kayaking through the mangroves** and over the turtle grass flats is one eco-tour all visitors to the Keys should appreciate. This is a good way to get an up-close look at bird nesting sites, sharks, stingrays, sea urchins, crabs, Florida crawfish and all manner of blowfish and other strange critters.

The very best time to enjoy a quiet paddle on the flats is at **daybreak or just before dark**. This is when a lot of fishy activity begins. It's feeding

SPORTS & RECREATION

MANGROVES

Mangroves are an amazing family of trees that grow on saltwater shorelines, their roots in the tidal water. A mangrove swamp is a unique ecosystem. The underwater forest of their roots makes a perfect habitat for barnacles, oysters, sponges, and sea squirts, which filter their food from the water as the tide goes in and out. Adolescent **fish** (including snook, snapper, shark, sea trout, tarpon and bonefish), shrimp, lobsters and many other creatures find shelter and food among the mangrove roots. **Birds** and **raccoons** live in the trees. Mangrove wetlands have **many ecological benefits**. They prevent coastal erosion, filter out pollutants, and absorb some of the wave energy of storm surges caused by hurricanes.

time for some of the big boys like snapper, grouper, bonefish, sharks and permit. Drift-

ing and paddling slowly around the miles and miles of turtle grass flats is a wonderful experience.

The **currents can be quite strong**, especially near bridges and in the channels between small keys or sand banks. If you time things right, you can plan your kayak trips to straddle a change in the tides. You can drift out on the last of the outgoing tide and drift back in when the tide changes and starts to come back in. Try to plan your trips so you drift with the tide instead of fighting against it.

Paddling in Florida Bay is excellent. There are hundreds of small mangrove keys to explore and hundreds of square miles of sand and turtle grass flats to drift over. Almost all of the area you can see on the Florida Bay side from the upper Keys is part of Everglades National Park.

On the ocean side, there are interesting patch reefs within a short paddle from shore. Due to the offshore reefs, the water is almost always fairly calm so paddlers can comfortably range up and down from Key Largo north to Elliot

Key and Sand Key. North of Key Largo receives few visitors and is a calm and relaxing area to explore. Watch the currents in the fascinating many channels of **Caesar's Creek.**

Any trips you make outdoors in the Keys require sunscreen, a hat and drinking water (beer, although also necessary, doesn't count). On a kayak or boat, you are soaking up even more sun than usual, because the reflection from the water almost doubles your exposure to the effects of the sun.

Lots of places rent kayaks or lead kayak tours. Many lodges offer them to guests for free. Here are a few of my favorites:

John Pennekamp Coral Reef State Park
From 8am until 3:45pm, you can rent kayaks at park headquarters at the marina. They have a choice of single or double sit-on sea kayaks. Basic safety equipment is provided. Prices range from $12 to $17 per hour. It is essential to reserve in advance. *Info: Key Largo, MM 102.5 OS. www.pennekamppark.com; Tel. 305-451-6300.*

Robbie's Boat Rentals
Robbie's is basically a marina where you can rent small boats and kayaks. They also organize trips to nearby **Indian Key** and **Lignumvitae Key.** It's at the base of a bridge near the tiny (10 acres) **Indian Key State Park** and other interesting places to paddle around. There are miles and miles of great flats and mangrove labyrinths to explore close by. *Info: MM 77.5 BS. Tel. 305-664-9814.*

Florida Bay Outfitters
Florida Bay Outfitters rents canoes and several types of kayaks—tandem, fishing, seagoing. They can set you up for a day or several weeks either on your own or on fully guided tours. *Info: MM 104 BS, Key Largo. www.kayakfloridakeys.com; Tel. 305-451-3018.*

MOTORCYCLING
There's only one road to drive on, but it's a beauty. Due to the popularity of the area and various Key West bike-related events, area businesses are biker-savvy. The tourism businesses in the Keys know bikers spend money.

M.D. Custom Cycles
This is the only place to rent

SPORTS & RECREATION

bikes in the Upper Keys. The Harleys go for about $125 per day. They also rent by the hour. You must reserve in advance and let them swipe your credit card for a deposit. *Info: Key Largo, MM 102.6. Tel. 305-451-3606.*

4. THE MIDDLE KEYS

HIGHLIGHTS

▲ Walking the old bridges and deserted beaches

▲ Kayak through the mangroves

▲ Diving Sombrero Key to spot mountains of coral and big barracuda

▲ Fishing for snapper and billfish

INTRO

Marathon, the Seven Mile Bridge, Sombrero Key, Florida Bay and the coral reefs fringing the Gulf Stream are what keep visitors coming back to the Middle Keys area. Just past Islamorada, the drive along the **Overseas Highway** becomes one of the most scenic drives anywhere in the world.

COORDINATES

Marathon, the commercial center of the **Middle Keys** has fast food and strip malls and a small airport but somehow retains its own charm. Lush coral reefs lie just offshore. The Middle Keys run from **MM 60 to MM 45**, the Seven Mile Bridge.

Make a leisurely drive down from Miami admiring the spectacular views out to sea from the bridges of the Overseas Highway, and check into one of the wonderful, quiet waterfront resorts. Spend most of your days out on the water: dive, fish, and kayak through the mangroves. In the evenings, indulge yourself shamelessly in seafood and umbrella drink consumption. Gorge on shrimp, lobster and stone crab.

The small town of **Marathon** is the gateway to the reefs of the Atlantic and the extensive sand and turtle grass flats of Florida Bay. The area has a quiet, laid-back feeling. Residents from up and down the Keys come here to shop at K-Mart. There is nightlife, but the screaming hordes of spring break party animals and other tourist hordes mostly pass this peaceful area by in favor of the more fleshy delights of Key West.

Fresh seafood and live music at the Hurricane – beer, live bands and fresh, steamed shrimp. It doesn't get much better.

THE MIDDLE KEYS IN A DAY

The Middle Keys are a bit of a long haul for a day trip from Miami, but if you leave very early in the morning and drive back wet and tired late at night, you'll have time for some sightseeing or an afternoon of kayaking, fishing or diving.

Morning
From Miami, take the Florida Turnpike or Krome Avenue

SIGHTS

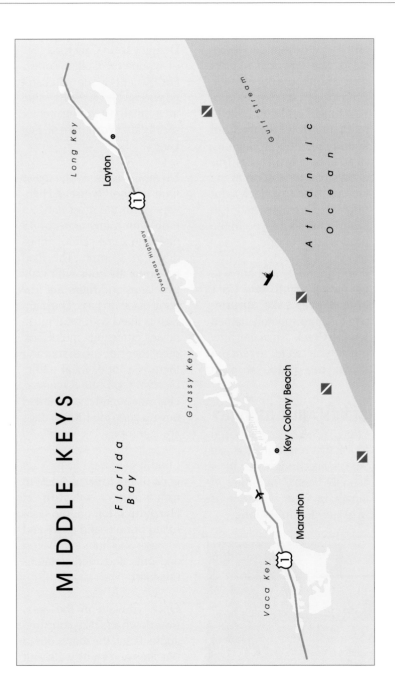

MIDDLE KEYS

Florida Bay

Atlantic Ocean

Gulf Stream

Long Key

Layton

Overseas Highway

Grassy Key

Key Colony Beach

Vaca Key

Marathon

SIGHTS

all the way to the end at Homestead. See *Practical Matters* for the best route out of town. Even though it takes 15 minutes longer and you have to pay a small toll, take the **Card Sound** route to Key Largo instead of staying on US 1. This allows you to stop off at the famous **Alabama Jack's** for tropical beverages and fish sandwiches to get you in the proper Keys mood.

If you are really in a hurry to get further south, take US 1 instead over **Lake Surprise** and the unfortunately named **Jewfish Creek**. No matter how much you want to get on down the road, stop at

SEVEN-MILE BRIDGE?

Oops. You're not supposed to ask that question. The *old* Seven Mile Bridge may have actually been 7 full miles in length but the new one is (whisper) **6.8 miles long**.

Denny's Latin Café for a shot of wonderful Cuban coffee. For 80 cents a cup you can't go wrong. It's on the Bay side in a small shopping center shortly after you arrive on Key Largo.

Drive Slowwwww! The speed limit on the Overseas Highway is, for the most part, 55 mph with a few areas of 45 mph and some school zones down to 30 mph. The road has long stretches with only two lanes and there are few good places to pass. The highway is lined with small businesses, attractions, motels and other roadside urban stuff and there is a lot of local traffic. Hurrying on the Overseas Highway is rarely possible and never a good idea. Radar traps are common.

I find it very hard to pass up good places to eat, even if I'm not hungry, so stop at **Harriette's** for an old-fashioned biscuits and gravy and sausage and ham and bacon and grits and fried potatoes breakfast.

Once you are in the area, slow down and take your time appreciating the views out to sea. Stop and enjoy walks out

on the abandoned Flagler railroad bridges with the fishermen and birders. You will almost certainly see sharks, stingrays, crabs and schools of brightly colored fish. Bridge walks are good at the bridges near MM60, **Duck Key**. The **Seven Mile Bridge** on the west side of Marathon is one of the very best.

A half-day diving trip is an excellent way to spend a morning. The huge coral formations at **Sombrero Key** are some of the most impressive I have seen anywhere. It is basically an enormous tongue and groove system with skyscraper-sized blocks of coral separated by white sand bottoms. The biggest barracuda on the planet lurks around. He'll follow you while slowly opening and closing his mouth full of wicked-looking teeth. Some say he is telling divers to bugger off. **Aquatic Adventures Dive Center** behind the Holiday Inn can set you up with a half-day, two-tank dive. Call ahead for reservations.

Afternoon
The best lunch spot in Marathon is undoubtedly **Castaway's**. It's a bit hard to find, but turn towards the ocean at MM 47.8 and start looking for the signs. They are appropriately located right next to the commercial fishing docks.

Island Tiki is also good. Kids love it but don't let them run around too much, as it would be easy for toddlers to tump over the railing into the bay. Barracudas and other kid lovers wait in the water for just this sort of thing to happen.

If fishing is your pleasure, you'll be glad to know that

SIGHTS

ALTERNATE PLAN

There is excellent kayaking on the sand flats and through the mangroves right around Marathon. **Marathon Kayak** can help you with rental equipment, and even has guided tours for those smart enough to reserve in advance.

you're in one of the most interesting fishing areas in the country. Flats fishing for bonefish, snapper and permit is excellent. Reef fishing for yellowtail and grouper can be had by going along with **Sea Dog Charters**, a party boat that supplies you with everything you need: tackle, bait, drinks, and fish. They'll even bait your hook for you, take the fish off when you get it in and clean it for ready for the pan. All for a mere $60 for the afternoon. What a deal!

Two Conchs Dive & Fishing Charters takes anglers offshore for the big ones in their 31-foot custom Contender or into the back areas of Florida Bay for bones and tarpon. A half-day trip costs around $500.

Sandy beaches are rare in the Keys, but there is a fairly nice one in Marathon. **Sombrero Beach Park** is a "public" beach, which means it has all sorts of BBQ facilities, swing sets, and volleyball stuff.

Evening
Captain's Three is a little pricey and only open for dinner, but still consistently good. There is a little bit of Old Keys charm left in the place.

If you can handle it, the **Hurricane Lounge & Restaurant** is *the* place to go for live music on weekends. They have cold beer and good seafood and Italian dishes. I'll never forget the time I caught **Rock Bottom** here. They rocked until late at night.

It's a long drive back to Miami and the highway is narrow. With the kids asleep in the back and the trunk full of wet towels, get your wife to sing to you as you blast through the night back to Miami. Better yet, let her drive. Try not to have a head-on collision. Stop at **Denny's** in Key Largo for a couple of shots of Cuban coffee to make the trip go easier.

A WEEKEND IN THE MIDDLE KEYS

A long weekend in the Marathon area is a great way to get away from the city. The drive down is short enough to get you into your hotel around sunset if you leave Miami fairly promptly after work on Friday. You'll have plenty of time for a wonderful seafood dinner followed by rockin' the night away to live music.

Friday Evening
From Miami, take the Florida Turnpike or Krome Avenue all the way to the end. See *Practical Matters* for the best route out of town. Krome Avenue is reasonably fast and is free. The Turnpike is almost always quicker but there is a substantial toll.

The Card Sound route to Key Largo takes slightly longer and there is a modest toll, but you get to stop for a soothing beverage and conch fritters at notorious **Alabama Jack's**, just before the bridge. Jack's is a funky swamp-side bar (bring your insect repellant into the bar with you) that specializes in being a funky swamp-side bar. The drinks come in plastic cups. Most of the drinks you'll have in the Keys come in plastic cups. Stopping at

Jack's is a good way to get yourself in the mood for the plastic cup bars you'll be visiting for the next few days. Make sure someone in your party doesn't drink too much.

The drive down past Key Largo is one of the most scenic drives anywhere in the world. The colorful, pastel contrasts between water, sand, sky and land are spectacular. Drive slowly. Enjoy the view. It's difficult to drive very fast in the Keys anyway and the cops are generous with speeding tickets.

Check into one of several fine resorts, such as the **Cocoplum Beach & Tennis Club**. It's right on the ocean, laid-back and

quiet. **The Sea Dell** is a 50s-style Mom and Pop motel that has been well cared for. It's not upscale, but costs half

SIGHTS

what some other places do and is very clean and nice. It is by far the nicest of the budget lodgings in the Keys. See *Best Sleeps & Eats* for more details on these and other resorts and hotels.

My favorite dinner spot is **Castaway's**, located on the road that turns towards the ocean at MM 47.8. Big piles of steamed shrimp washed down by ice-cold imported beer, grouper, yellowtail and Florida crawfish top the menu.

Saturday Morning

There are two great places for breakfast. The **Seven Mile Grille** is right at the Marathon end of the famous bridge, and serves great breakfast stuff, burgers, seafood and Mexican specials. The steamed shrimp deal is a good choice. The beer is cold. The Key lime pie is some of the best. The wonderful ladies running the place are friendly but won't take any crap from customers. Be sure you don't offer any.

The other breakfast spot is the local greasy spoon called the **Wooden Spoon**. It's actually not so greasy and the corned beef hash is superb. There are wooden spoons hung all over the walls for some reason. All the local cops and charter captains eat here in the morning. You should too.

There is plenty to do in the Middle Keys, and you have one full day, Saturday, and most of Sunday to do it. The offshore coral reefs are the most spectacular attraction of the Keys, and the way to enjoy them is by diving and fishing. A half-day, two-tank dive with a dive operator like **Reef Runner** in Marathon will take you to reefs like the shallow but spectacular **Delta Shoal** or **Sombrero Key**. The coral formations at both sites are enormous. Look for the huge 'cuda at Sombrero.

Marathon is one of the main sport fishing centers in the Keys and the choice of charter captains is broad. Offshore charter boats run from $450 to over $1,000 per day. Stroll along the docks in the evening and see which boats seem to be doing the best. The marina at the Holiday Inn has a few charter boats you can check on. **Pursuit Fishing** and **Adios Charters** are two of the better-known operations for offshore sails and dorado (mahi).

Flats and mangrove fishing for bones, snook, snapper and tarpon is at its best in this area. Good charter captains will find the fish for you and show you how to hook 'em, catch 'em and get 'em in the boat. If you really want to catch a mess of fish and don't want to pay hundreds of dollars, a party boat such as the **Marathon Lady** costs only about $60 for a full day. They give you all the equipment and bait you need to bottom fish on the reefs for snapper and grouper. What a deal!

Two Conchs Dive & Fishing Charters takes anglers offshore for the big ones in their three 31-foot custom Contenders, or into the back areas of Florida Bay for bones and tarpon. A half-day goes for around $500.

Bonefish are notoriously hard to find and catch. The activity is all about "fishing" for them, which is great fun. It's not about "catching" them. Whenever anglers in the Keys return to the dock at the end of the day with no fish they are usually quick to explain: "we were fishing for bones." Bystanders immediately understand and sympathize.

These guys weren't actually *planning* on catching any fish anyway.

Saturday Afternoon
The lunch choices are great, as long as you're in the mood for seafood (and I almost always am). **Burdines** is a seafood-in-a-basket kind of place. Their shrimp and grouper are excellent. This is a good spot to drink beer and enjoy bar snacks. They sometimes have bands on the weekends.

Keys Fisheries is probably the best lunch spot. It's in a marina and doesn't amount to much more than a window where you place your order, and a few picnic tables. That's fine. The food is terrific. Try

SIGHTS

the lobster Reuben sandwich. Delicious!

Both **Booth Key** and **Cocoplum Beach** are good kayak spots. You can park and launch easily and enjoy meandering through back passages in the mangroves and along the shallow reefs just offshore. **Marathon Kayak** can rent you equipment or take you on a guided tour.

The beach at **Cocoplum Beach** is not the pristine white sand and curling, surfable breakers you may have enjoyed in other parts of Florida. The Keys just don't have fancy tourist beaches. The beaches they do have are what I call "interesting" beaches in that they tend to be rocky, covered with weird stuff tossed up by storms, and fringed by mangroves packed with exotic bird species. **Sombrero Beach Park** is made up mostly of imported sand but it is a nice spot for the kids. There are playground facilities, picnic areas and all the usual city park-type amenities.

You simply must take the time to walk out onto the old **Seven Mile Bridge**. You can park just past the Seven Mile Grille and walk waaay out over the shallow flats enjoying sightings of horseshoe crabs, bull sharks and leopard rays as they meander their way across the shallow sand and turtle grass flats. The water is almost always surprisingly clear, and you are up high as you stroll along, so you get a great view of all the fishy action. The bridge almost always has a few hard-core bridge fishermen enjoying a cheap day out. Bridge walks are one of my favorite Keys activities. Bring sunscreen and a hat.

ALTERNATE PLAN

Lounge around the pool all day Saturday enjoying refreshing tropical beverages. A couple of half-hour snorkel excursions in the shallow water in front of the resort can be followed by more pool time. Venture into town in the evening to gorge on seafood and enjoy some live music at the **Hurricane**.

Saturday Evening

Dinner offers more possibilities for funky seafood joints, but don't pass up a chance for a little fine dining. Many people like **Cabot's** for its slightly snooty atmosphere.

The food is good, but the prices are a little high. It's not my favorite.

The **Barracuda Grill** is a little on the pricey side, but the seafood and steaks are good. They have a nice wine list— also on the pricey side. The atmosphere is remodeled Old Florida. It's one of my favorites.

Nightlife in the middle keys means beverages and bands at the **Hurricane**, followed by more beverages and fun at the late-night **Brass Monkey**. The Hurricane has blues bands Thursday through Saturday, starting around 9:30.

Things start cooking at the **Brass Monkey** about 2:00 in the morning, after things wind down at the Hurricane (locals say "it's about monkey-thirty"). This is a simple bar in the Kmart shopping center. Local tourism workers come here after work to party until dawn.

Sunday

If you feel like your life simply will not be worth living if you do not get to frolic with dolphins, then you should arrange in advance to visit to the so-called **Dolphin Research Center**. This is where the whole **Flipper** thing supposedly started. For a mere $155, punters are allowed to sit in on educational dolphin talks and spend a few minutes in the water with captive dolphins. Keep in mind these dolphins are captive.

Even though the word "research" is in the name of the place, the only "research" I can see going on is studying how to move dollars from tourist pockets into the attraction owners' pockets. Real dolphin researchers feel that any facility with captive dolphins charging the public to come in and fool around with them is definitely *not* a serious research organization but is merely another roadside attraction; one that relies on imprisoning free-ranging wild dolphins for their profit.

All ages must pay the full price and an adult, who must also pay the full price, must accompany small children. So your total will come out to somewhere north of $500 after T-shirts, DVDs and soft drinks. What a deal.

Sunday evening you can give

SIGHTS

up early and head back to Miami while it's still light out, or party on and make the long drive back in the dark. The roads are two-lane in many areas, so be very careful driving. Head-on collisions happen.

Drive Slowwwww! The speed limit on the Overseas Highway is, for the most part, 55 mph with a few areas of 45 mph and some school zones down to 30 mph. The road has long stretches with only two lanes, and there are few good places to pass. The highway is lined with small businesses, attractions, motels and other roadside urban stuff and there is a lot of local traffic. Hurrying on the Overseas Highway is rarely possible and never a good idea. Radar traps are common.

Stop by **Denny's** in Key Largo for great Cuban coffee to keep you awake. If you need just one more visit to a funky bar, take the Card Sound route back from Key Largo and stop by **Alabama Jack's** for yet more of your favorite tropical beverages and one more grouper sandwich. Be sure to try the conch fritters.

A WEEK IN THE MIDDLE KEYS

The Middle Keys offer not only **one of the finest scenic drives in North America**, but also some of the very best fishing and certainly the very best diving. In spite of their fame and beauty, the Middle Keys are not a heavily touristed area. The Keys in general are not particularly built up — few high-rise condos meet the eye. Sure, there are plenty of cheesy roadside attractions and souvenir shops, but the atmosphere in general is very laid-back and non-urban. The attractions are funky tiki bars, seafood feasts, hilarious holiday bar bands, fishing, diving and having fun. The waters around the Keys are filled with sea life, making the ocean by far the most spectacular attraction of them all.

Day One
The **Marathon** area is about 100 miles or so from Miami, but the drive can take much longer than you might think. Traffic in Miami can be tough, but the lines of cars into the

Keys on Friday afternoons and out again on Sunday evenings can be maddening. The **Overseas Highway** is only two lanes for much of its length. It's not the kind of road you are going to go very fast on even when there isn't much traffic. Radar enforcement of speed limits is frequent.

I like to stay in quiet places but still near the action if possible, so when I'm in the Middle Keys area my favorite place to stay is the **Cocoplum**. It's just outside Marathon on the Atlantic side, kind of off by itself on the waterfront. They have weird but particularly nice round cottages with full amenities for a weeklong stay. The beach nearby is actually fairly sandy and nice for long walks. The location is quiet. They have a pool and tennis courts. Ask about kayaking in the vicinity.

The best budget motel in the Keys is **Sea Dell**. The Sea Dell is a '50s-style motel that has been lovingly maintained. The landscaping is super and the pool pleasant.

Most Keys eateries are casual places with pretty much the same menu items for lunch or

LOBSTER?

What you see on menus in the Keys called "lobster" is actually a delicious critter known officially as a **Florida crawfish** or, locally, "lobster." The lobster served in Florida (*panulirus argus*, aka spiny lobster, crawfish, or bug) is a different species from the Maine lobster (*homarus americanus*) found in colder waters. Their claws are tiny and only the scrumptious tail is eaten. Wonderful! Don't miss it!

dinner. Good lunch selections include the **Seven Mile Grille**, **Castaway's**, **Blond Giraffe** (for its great Key Lime pie), **Island Tiki** – for my complete list, see *Best Sleeps & Eats* later in this chapter.

Days Two - Six
Snorkeling and scuba diving conditions in the Middle Keys area are the best in the US. There are miles of reefs with drop-offs, caves, sandy chan-

SIGHTS

nels and all manner of exotic reef fish. The edge of the **Gulf Stream** is immediately adjacent to the outer reefs; bringing pelagic creatures close in for your viewing (and fishing) pleasure.

Perhaps the most impressive area of reefs is directly off Marathon. **Sombrero Key** is a series of huge coral mounds the size of freight trains or small skyscrapers lying on their sides. It covers hundreds of acres and ranges from only inches deep to drop-offs into the blue of the Gulf Stream. Sand channels separate the coral structures and a plethora of dazzling reef fish flit about.

Discount Divers and **Aquatic Adventures Dive Center** are two good choices for full- or half-day diving or snorkeling trips in boats with no more than six divers.

There is an utterly colossal barracuda called "**Pokey**" that hangs out around the Sombrero Key reefs. Some 8 or 10 feet long, Pokey has enormous teeth and likes to glide around his domain slowly opening and closing his mouth. He shadows worried scuba divers as they tour the area, but I've never heard of him actually attacking anyone. He is waaay too formidable for you to think about attempting to feed him.

The wreck of the 200-foot **Thunderbolt** is one of the better wreck dives in the Keys. It's sitting on the 115-foot bottom pretty much upright. There is still quite a lot of structure and much interior exploring to do if you are up to it. It is deep and close to the Gulf Stream so you may see large tuna, amberjack or even the occasional sailfish swimming by. Pay attention.

Not far from the Thunderbolt, **Coffins Patch** is a series of coral mounds or "patches" surrounded by sandy areas. It is a shallow dive and good for a last dive of the day. Several Spanish treasure ships foundered here and the remains of some can still be seen. Look for gold coins and emerald jewelry.

Fishing in the Middle Keys happens to be some of the best in North America. It also happens to be a great excuse to get out on the water and view the beauty of the Keys from the best angle.

Florida Bay and **Everglades National Park** are just a little bit out on the bay side. As you look out over Florida Bay, most of the mangrove islands you see off in the distance are within the boundaries of Everglades National Park.

The shallow Florida Bay is made up of hundreds of square miles of sand and turtle grass flats threaded with deep channels. The area is home to the elusive **bonefish, permit** and **tarpon** (the **Silver King**). The typical fishing boat in this area is a small outboard-powered skiff with a high platform at the stern, which the guide uses to pole the boat around and look for signs of fishy activity. This is great fun even if you don't catch any fish

(fortunately, such an occurrence is rare). A kayak is another great way to enjoy fishing on the flats.

One of my favorite ways to spend an afternoon or two is to go **bridge and bank fishing**, roaming from bridge to bridge, drowning shrimp and pinfish. Properly equipped with a loaded cooler, wide-brimmed hat, polarized sunglasses, sunscreen, candy bars and a good assortment of my favorite fishing lures, I'm ready for hours of fun.

My usual plan is to start out the day by popping quickly under the east end of the short bridge just east of the airport. There is a crummy little park there where you can park (keep a close eye on your vehicle here). You are basically fishing from the rip-rap under the bridge with the current blazing by in one direction or the other and with

SIGHTS

boats blasting by all the time, but I've nailed a couple of nice **grouper** at this spot. A deep-diving plug or one-ounce tipped jig is good in this situation.

I only fish this spot for a half-hour at most, then head east to try my luck at the bridges around **Duck Key**. There are several short bridges you can try with variations of flats and channels. Most people like to fish on the side with the current running away from the bridge so their lines don't get messed up on the pilings under the bridges. I prefer the other side, letting my heavily weighted bait go down deep under the bridge with the current. I believe the big 'uns are waiting behind the bridge pilings, out of the current, hoping for something, like my bait, to come drifting along.

If I catch a small "trash" fish I may be so bold as to stick it on a large circle hook with a steel leader, a heavy weight and 30-pound test line. I drop this puppy over the side, set a light drag with the clicker on and sit back to enjoy a cold beverage, hoping for something interesting to come along.

I don't always have the patience for this technique to pay off, but now and then I haul in something large this way: **sharks, rays, grouper**, even an over-30-pound **snapper** one night. The cold beverage part is the secret ingredient.

I usually sample a couple of spots around **Duck Key** before moving on to the bridges around **Long Key**. There are some interesting channels near the **Long Key State Park**. The usual selection of bait - shrimp, small baitfish, plugs and heavy jigs - works well for me. If I find a spot I like, I may actually bring the cooler out onto the bridge with me, but I usually only spend a half hour or so in any one spot and leave the cooler in the truck. I like to keep moving, as I'm sure my fishing luck will be better at the next spot. You should have been here yesterday.

At this point it's best to head back west towards Marathon again. If any of the previous bridges were particularly productive or otherwise interesting, it might be wise to check them again quickly on the way back. Next stop: **Seven Mile Bridge**.

The Seven Mile Bridge is a little higher than some of the other bridges but it covers some interesting territory and the walkable part is quite long. The far end, the west end of the bridge, is my favorite bridge fishing spot anywhere. There are great flats and some deep channels. You can cast under the new bridge as well as the one you are walking on. There is good parking. The **Seven Mile Grille** waits patiently at the end of the bridge, just past the parking lot. They have cold beer and wonderful bar food.

This is a sure spot to land one of those pesky barracudas. Cuda are good fighters and put on a good show jumping out of the water and tail walking. Don't lose your finger trying to take the hook out of a barracuda's mouth. Just cut the line.

Offshore fishing is huge in Keys. There are dozens of charter boats ready to take you out for mahi, kings, sailfish or marlin.

Not just for po' boys, **party boats** are great if you want to get out on the reefs and fish without spending hundreds of dollars. Both the **Marathon Lady** at $35 and **Sea Dog Charters** at $60 supply everything you need for a half-day fishing on the reefs, except your favorite beverages. The crew of the Marathon Lady will go so far as to bait your hook for you and drop it in the water if you need that much help. **Almost everyone catches fish.** The crew will even clean them for you (a small tip is customary for this service). The Sea Dog is not quite as crowded as the Marathon Lady. It's best to make reservations for either boat.

There are dozens of fishing guides and charter boats as well as a couple of party boats in the area.

Marathon happens to have two of the best beaches in the Keys. On the ocean side at the west end of Marathon, **Sombrero Beach** is accessible through the public park and offers a mile or so of fairly uninterrupted **beachcombing** pleasure. The water is shallow and perhaps **good for beginning snorkelers**. At the other end of town, Coco Plum Beach is usually deserted. This is a good place to **bird watch** for terns.

SIGHTS

One of the very best nature walks in the Keys is to be had merely by walking out on the old abandoned **Seven Mile Bridge**. You can walk for a mile or so with a great view of the shallow turtle grass and sand flats and the deep channels separating them. You will almost certainly see dozens of odd sea creatures such as horseshoe crabs, nurse sharks and leopard rays, and you might just see a couple of huge tarpon moving through the channel.

One of the best things about bridge walks is the opportunity to watch and chat with the anglers who hang out on the old bridges wetting a line. It is not impolite to peer in their buckets and inspect their catch as you walk past.

The wonderfully touristy **Key West** is within reach of the Middle Keys for a great day trip. It would be best to hustle on down early in the morning to beat the traffic a little and to give yourself the most time possible in Key West.

The drive over the **Seven Mile Bridge** and on down through the Keys to Key West is one of my favorite drives in North America. The views out to sea are brilliant. There a couple of places worth a quick stop on the way down, even if you do want to hurry to Key West.

Bahía Honda State Park has one of the best beaches in the Keys, and you should take a

short stroll absorbing the solitude. You can see freighters chugging along out at the edge of the Gulf Stream, and the looming, old abandoned bridge is a haunting sight.

Go *reeeaaaal* slow through the Keys around **Big Pine**. You might see a **Key deer** if you are lucky. The cops watch for speeders in this area and, if you hit a Key deer, you're definitely going to hell.

Baby's Coffee at MM 15 OS is a good place to power-slam a latte before getting into Key West.

Be aware that there is only one road in and out of Key West and the law enforcement authorities realize that many people who have been visiting the fine drinking establishments just mentioned will be heading out of town at the end of the evening for the long trip back to Miami or other parts of the Keys. This means occasional **sobriety roadblocks** on the Overseas Highway. Make sure you have a driver who has not been drinking.

Last Day

It's a pretty long haul back to Miami, but don't worry about that until late afternoon— there's still plenty to do. Snag a quick breakfast at the **Wooden Spoon** or the **Seven Mile Grille**. If they pack a lunch for you, that will mean more time to spend having fun on the water.

The Middle Keys are a terrific area to enjoy from a kayak. There are **hundreds of small mangrove islands** within paddling distance of the highway. Of particular note is the area around **Coco Plum Beach**. All around the ocean side of the island, you can find paddling routes through the mangroves and over the grass flats. There are dozens of docks to throw plugs at. Expect huge snook, snapper and the occasional grouper.

Marathon Kayak at MM 50 OS in Sombrero Resort can set you up with everything you need. Most of their kayaks are the easy-to-use sit-on type. You can get **lessons** and go on **guided tours** with these guys.

The very best time to enjoy a quiet paddle on the flats is at daybreak or just before dark. This is when a lot of fishy activity begins. It's feeding time for some of the big boys like snapper, grouper, bonefish, sharks and permit. Drifting and paddling slowly around the miles and miles of turtle grass flats is a wonderful experience.

The currents can be quite strong, especially near bridges and in the channels between small keys or sand banks. If you time things right, you can plan your kayak trips to straddle a change in the tides. You can drift out on the last of the outgoing tide and drift back in when the tide changes and starts to come back in.

SIGHTS

Try to plan your trips so you drift with the tide instead of fighting against it.

Any trips you make outdoors in the Keys require sunscreen, a hat and drinking water (beer, although also necessary, doesn't count). On a kayak or boat you are soaking up even more sun than usual, because the reflection from the water almost doubles your exposure to the effects of the sun.

On the way back to Miami, stop and have dinner at the **Whale Harbor Inn**. The enormous seafood buffet is world famous. This is not just another steam table joint. They have shrimp, crab, squid, prime rib, and the entire usual buffet stuff, but top quality and more of it. We always stopped here for dinner when I was a kid.

Drive back to Miami in the dark with a backseat full of sleeping kids and wet bathing suits, and try not to have a head-on collision.

BEST SLEEPS & EATS

SLEEPS & EATS

BEST OF THE BEST IN THE MARATHON KEYS
Cocoplum Beach & Tennis Club $$$$

This unique property is located just outside Marathon, on a small strip of sand that will have to pass

for a sandy "beach" in the Keys. It's quiet and peaceful, and you can stroll quite a ways down the beach. The units are large, two bedroom, round structures clustered together with lots of exotic tropical plants, tennis courts and a pool. All the units have full kitchen facilities. If you plan on staying in the area for a few days or a week, this would be a great choice. *Info: MM 54.5 OS, Marathon. www.cocoplum.com; Tel. 305-743-0240.*

Sea Dell Motel $

This is a plain ol' mom and pop style 1950s motel, but it's nicely kept up, clean and one of the few bargains in the Keys. It's on the main drag just up from the Hurricane. They have a pool, morning coffee in the office and small refrigerators in the rooms. Pets are welcome. It's not fancy but I like it. *Info: MM 50 BS, Marathon. www.seadellmotel.com. Tel. 305-743-5161.*

Gulf View Waterfront Resort $$

Almost everyone who stays at this small resort (only 11 units) has great things to say. The rooms have kitchens, the grounds are quiet and tropical, and the pool is clean and refreshing. They have kayaks and canoes available free for guests, and the Dolphin Research Lab is right next door so you can get a good feel for what's happening over the fence in case you want to participate. It's one of the better bargains in the area. They offer wireless Internet, putting green, boat launch and numerous other amenities. *Info: MM 58.5, Grassy Key. www.gulfviewwaterfrontresort.com; Tel. 305-289-1414.*

Seven Mile Grille $

This is one of the great Keys landmarks. Breakfast is legendary (corned beef hash, blueberry pancakes!). Chili, steamed shrimp, burgers, seafood, conch fritters and chowder, all sorts of crab dishes and wonderful fish sandwiches are the deal. They have great breakfasts. The steamed shrimp is a good choice. The beer is cold. The Key lime pie is some of the best. The wonderful ladies running the place are friendly, but won't take any crap from customers. Be sure you don't offer any. It's not at all fancy but the cooking is homestyle, the staff is effici-

MIDDLE KEYS DINING

For me, the most important part of any guidebook is the part that describes the restaurants. Seafood is on the menu at almost every eatery in the Keys. **Marathon** and the areas around it are filthy with places to enjoy **local shrimp, Florida crawfish** (lobster to you), **yellowtail, grouper** and other exotic fish specialties. Lunch or dinner. You can have it in a plastic basket with wax paper or on fine china with linen tablecloths. I believe I have tried every place to eat in the area at least once. The restaurants listed here are my favorites.

ent and the location is handy if you've been out strolling or fishing on the bridge. I always feel a bit put out if I somehow fail to eat here on a trip to the Keys. *Info: MM 47 BS, Marathon. Tel. 305-743-4481.*

Barracuda Grill $$$$

Open only for dinner, the Barracuda is a little more upscale than most of the nearby eateries. One glance at the prices on the wine list (fairly comprehensive) tells you that. They have great steaks and even rack of lamb but they are justly famous for their seafood. Even though it has no particular ambiance, it is one of the most popular restaurants with non-budget Marathon visitors and locals. The service and food quality are consistent. I've visited several times and have always been very pleased. They've given some thought to the kid's menu—no unhealthy chicken nuggets. *Info: MM 49.5 BS, Marathon. www.barracudagrillmarathonfl.com; Tel. 305-743-3314.*

Burdine's $

If you like great, stonking, messy hamburgers this is the place. They also have good fish sandwiches and wonderful fries. Locals swear by it. It's not expensive. *Info: MM 48 OS, Marathon. www.burdineswaterfront.com, Tel. 305-743-5317.*

Captains Three

This is a seafood market, not a restaurant, but it is my family's favorite spot to buy fresh snapper, grouper, shrimp, mahi and other wonderful seafood whenever we are in the area and have cooking facilities in our lodging. If eating several pounds of fresh shrimp appeals to you, but you can't spend the $40 plus bucks it would take to do so in a restaurant, this is the way to go. *Info: MM 54.5 OS, Coco Plum Drive, Marathon. Tel. 305-289-1131.*

Castaway's $$$

It's a little hard to find, but Castaway's, the oldest restaurant in Marathon, is not to be missed. Turn towards the ocean side at MM 47.8 and head for the commercial fishing docks. Expect *very* fresh fish and shrimp and *very* cold beer. This is probably my favorite of the Old Keys seafood-in-a-basket joints. *Info: MM 47.8, 1406 Oceanview Ave., Marathon. Tel. 305-743-6247.*

Don Pedro's Cuban Restaurant $$

Don Pedro cooks what I have to call "Cuban influenced cuisine." They don't eat like this in Cuba—even in the very best hotels. He definitely has the imagination to come up with some interesting fusion dishes. Steak, local seafood and, of course, Cuban sandwiches are to be had. It's a little on the small side, so you may have to wait on busy nights. *Info: MM 53.5 OS, Marathon. Tel. 305-743-5247.*

Herbie's $$

If you're a tourist you'll probably love Herbie's. It's shamelessly tourist-oriented. In spite of this, you'll see plenty of locals slopping down brews and cocktails during happy hour. Sometimes there is live music and dancing. Wednesday night is the big night. *Info: MM 50 BS, Marathon. Tel. 305-743-6373.*

MARGARITAS

Everybody loves margritas and the Keys is where the art of their construction reaches its peak. Most of the margaritas you will try are made from a powder. Some bars even dispense the golden beverage from hoses into plastic cups. In the Keys, margaritas are almost always served in plastic cups. Proper margaritas are made from tequila, triple sec, lime juice, sugar and water. Most bars make them from tequila, powder and ice. On the rocks or slushie? The frozen concoction is simply wonderful but they tend to go down too easily. On the rocks, rocks.

SLEEPS & EATS

Hurricane Grille $$$

The Hurricane is a nice medium-priced restaurant serving seafood and Italian dishes. You can enjoy good seafood, chicken, steaks and pasta seated next to fantastic saltwater aquariums filled with dangerous but attractive ocean denizens. There are certainly better places to eat nearby but the Hurricane is also one of the better live music venues in the area. The band starts a bit after most people's dinner hour, but you can eat and enjoy the music at the same time. I love the place. *Info: MM 49.5 BS, Marathon. Tel. 305-743-2220.*

Island Tiki Bar & Restaurant $$

I like Island Tiki. This place is almost always packed with pushy tourists with carloads of screaming kids who just got out after a

SLEEPS & EATS

three hour drive and need to let off steam. The waterfront view is great and the food is fine. They have a full bar and all sorts of seafood—not just the local stuff. The open-air ambiance is great and the bar food and steamed shrimp are much better than average. They concoct a wide variety of rum drinks and have a good selection of beer. The place is right by the side of the road, and looks like just what it is: a typical Keys seafood bar. Don't come here if you can't handle a few kids. If you've got kids, try to keep them under lose control here, because there's a real danger of them pitching over the low rails and ending up in the drink. The water around the restaurant teems with barracuda, stingrays, nurse sharks. . .you get the idea. I like the place, even though the kids get to me sometimes. *Info: MM 54 BS, Marathon. Tel. 305-743-4191.*

Keys Fisheries $$

Turn a little past the Stuffed Pig (don't stop there) and follow your nose to yet another funky seafood joint on the dock in a marina. This is a simple place. Order food at one window, make up a name (must be a celebrity - I'm usually Muddy Waters) to be called by and order your drinks at a second window. Picnic tables complete the scene. They sometimes have all-you-can-eat crab deals. Good food—that's about it. *Info: Gulf View Ave., Marathon. Tel. 305-743-4353.*

The Quay $$

A lot of people rave about the Quay, but I am not particularly impressed. They do have $1 beers from time to time, but the place seems a bit of a sloppy mess to me. *Info: MM 54 BS, Marathon. Tel. 305-289-1810.*

Wooden Spoon $

This place has twee little wooden spoons hung all over the walls for some reason, but they serve fine food. This is one of the two best breakfast joints in the area - the corned beef hash is superb. All the local cops and charter captains eat here in the morning. You should too. Biscuits, gravy, grits, even corned beef hash compete for your daily allowance of cholesterol. Go for it. Take an extra Lipitor to make up for the sausage patties. *Info: Marathon. Tel. 305-743-8383.*

BEST SHOPPING

There aren't very many places to indulge in real shopping frenzies. You can buy T-shirts, wraps and cheesy tourist souvenirs at only a few places. If you're in the market for fishing tackle, you're all set. There are plenty of places to indulge your tackle-shopping fantasies. Gift shoppes come and go. Try these:

Driftwood Designs

Handcrafted jewelry, fine gifts. *Info: Marathon, Gulfside Village. Tel. 305-743-7591.*

Keyker's & Co.

Unique Clothing & gifts. *Info: Marathon. Tel. 305-743-0107.*

Museum of Crane Point Hammock

T-shirts, natural & sea life gift ideas. *Info: Marathon, MM 50.5. Tel. 305-743-9100.*

Sandpiper Loft

Ladies' apparel, swimsuits, dress and sportswear. *Info: Marathon. Tel. 305-743-3205.*

Captains Three

This is a seafood market—a favorite spot for my family to buy fresh snapper, grouper, shrimp, mahi and other wonderful seafood whenever we are in the area and have cooking facilities in our lodging. If eating several pounds of fresh shrimp appeals to you, but you can't spend the $40 +

SHOPPING

bucks it would take to do so in a restaurant, this is the way to go. *Info: MM 54.5 OS, Coco Plum Drive, Marathon. Tel. 305-289-1131.*

Key Bana Resort Apparel
A smart shop with name-brand resort ware and accessories. I hear the selection of swimsuits is splendid. *Info: Marathon, Key Colony Beach Shopping Center. Tel. 305-289-1161.*

BEST NIGHTLIFE & ENTERTAINMENT

Marathon boasts the **Hurricane Lounge**—a great venue for touring blues bands featuring live music, food and drink, and the **Brass Monkey**, a late-night place catering to locals and tourist trade workers. Other than that . . . the party's at your place.

Angler's Lounge
Live entertainment nightly. *Info: Marathon, MM 48.2 BS, in the Faro Blanco Resort. Tel. 305-743-9018.*

Hurricane Grille
The Hurricane is a nice medium-priced restaurant serving seafood and Italian dishes. You can enjoy good seafood, chicken, steaks and pasta seated next to fantastic salt-water aquariums filled with dangerous but attractive ocean denizens, then stroll into the bar for the live music, which takes place every weekend. I love the place. *Info: MM 49.5 BS, Marathon. Tel. 305-743-2220.*

Brass Monkey
Things start cooking at the **Brass Monkey** about 2 in the morning, after things wind down at the Hurricane (locals say "it's about monkey-thirty"). This is a simple bar frequented by local tourism workers who come after work to party until dawn. They also have a lively happy hour from 4-8. *Info: Marathon, in the K-Mart shopping center at the end of the building.*

NIGHTLIFE & ENTERTAINMENT

BEST SPORTS & RECREATION

DIVING & SNORKELING

Sombrero Key is probably the best-known dive site in the Middle Keys. It's not really a key at all, but just a shallow spot on the reef about six miles out with an enormous steel-frame lighthouse. You can see the lighthouse from the Seven Mile Bridge. The reef is close to the edge of the Gulf Stream, and consists of huge, sky-scraper-size chucks of living coral separated by narrow sand channels. It is basically an enormous tongue and groove reef system.

There is an utterly colossal barracuda called **"Pokey"** that hangs out around the Sombrero Key reefs. Some 8 or 10 feet long, Pokey has enormous teeth and likes to glide around his domain slowly opening and closing his mouth. He shadows worried scuba divers as they tour the area, but I've never heard of him actually attacking anyone. He is waaay too formidable for you to think about attempting to feed him.

The wreck of the 200-foot **Thunderbolt** is one of the better wreck dives in the Keys. It's sitting on the 115-foot bottom pretty much upright. There is still quite a lot of structure and much interior exploring if you are up to it. It is deep and close to the Gulf Stream so you may see large tuna, amberjack or even the occasional sailfish swimming by. Pay attention.

Not far from the Thunderbolt, **Coffins Patch** is a series of coral mounds or "patches" surrounded by sandy areas. It is a shallow dive and good for a last dive of the day. Several Spanish treasure ships foundered here and the remains of some can still be seen. Look for gold coins and emerald jewelry.

DRIFT DIVES

A relaxing way to see a lot of reef is by simply floating along with the current while your dive boat floats along with you. When there is a stiff current running and good visibility, you can cover quite a bit of reef and can sneak up on shy pelagics, turtles and rays.

SPORTS & RECREATION

Delta Shoal is a series of patch reefs in relatively shallow water that is a good choice for a shallow second or third dive.

There are dozens of scuba and snorkeling operators. Here are my favorites in the Middle Keys:

Abyss Dive Center

With small groups, Abyss visits over 50 different sites from shallow patch reefs to the wreck of the Thunderbolt. They have a full dive shop of

and lodging. Near the Holiday Inn. *Info: Marathon, MM 54. www.abyssdive.com; Tel. 305-743-2126.*

Reef Runner

These guys deliver real service for divers. They offer hotel pick-up and drop-off. They only run one trip per day, and customize the daily trip to meet the expectations their clients. Captain Sam

Watson visits four or five sites each trip, according to the desires and skill levels of the chartering party. They never have more than six divers on the boat. *Info: Marathon. www.floridadivecharter.com; Tel. 305-289-9808.*

Discount Divers

This is more than just a dive shop. These guys offer a full dive holiday with lodging, diving, equipment, instruction, and on and on. Their B&B has good deals for groups. Captain Ed Davidson has been running things for many years and is full of inter-

DIVE BUDDIES

It's a good idea to be sure the people you'll be diving with over a few days have similar interests and skill levels as yourself, so you won't spend your valuable vacation time diving in areas that hold little interest for you. I once spent two days diving with two guys from Boston who were only interested in caves. Caves are okay, but I prefer looking at coral and big fish, so a good old reef or wall dive suits me best. Needless to say, I am more careful now about selecting my dive companions.

esting local lore. *Info: MM 52 BS, Marathon. www.discount-diversbandb.com; Tel. 305-743-2400.*

FISHING

There are dozens of fishing guides and charter boats, as well as a couple of party boats in the area. Here are some of my favorites in the Middle Keys:

Two Conchs Dive & Fishing Charters

Two Conchs takes anglers off-shore for the big ones in Captain Jack Carlson's 31-foot custom Contender, or into the back areas of Florida Bay for bones and tarpon. A half day trip goes for around $500. *Info: Marathon. www.twoconchs.com; Tel. 305-743-6253.*

Catch 'Em All Charters

This outfit runs a 28-foot custom Parker with twin 150hp Yamahas, which is a good size for both inshore and off-shore action. It's fast, so you'll get to the hot spots quickly for more time with your hook in the water. This is important. They'll take you trolling for billfish and dorado (mahi) or bottom bumping for Goliath grouper and amberjack. A full day runs around $800 de-pending on the time of year. *Info: Marathon. www.catch-em-all.com; Tel. 305-481-4568.*

Marathon Lady

Trips on the Marathon Lady go for $30 for a half day with bait and $5 for tackle rental. Not bad. They take you out to the patch reefs to bottom fish for snapper, grouper and tasty yellowtail. The occasional shark or barracuda keeps things interesting. *Info: MM 53, Vaca Cut Bridge. www.marathonlady.com; Tel. 305-743-5580.*

Sea Dog Charters

This party boat offers morning, afternoon and night fishing trips for $60 per person. You get all the bait and tackle you need, and they show you how to do it. Bring your own drinks and food. It's very rare that someone doesn't catch any fish. They'll clean them for you at the end of the trip. This operation takes a smaller group than most party boats. It's not a cattle boat at all and the price is right. *Info: MM 47.5 BS, Near the Seven Mile Grille. Tel. 305-743-8255.*

BOATING

Renting a car while on vacation in an unfamiliar area is a great way to see the sights around you. Renting a boat in the Keys is much the same (as long as you know what you're doing). The best things about the Keys are in the water and you need a boat to get to them.

There is a wide variety of boat rental operators. Check their web sites and call in advance to be sure they have the type of boat and equipment you need. Be sure to reserve well in advance. Some rental operators will deliver the boat if you are renting for several days.

A word of warning: boating in

the Keys is not like driving. There are no street signs or stop signs. Sand bars and reefs pop up unexpectedly. Damage to props on rental boats is routine. There are extremely stiff fines for damaging coral or sand and grass flats with your boat or its propeller. The fines are calculated by the square inch of damage to the bottom. Damage to the bottom of your boat is a matter between you and the rental operator. Unless you know what you're doing, do your boating with guides, in their boats.

Captain Pip's

The marina here rents 18-24-foot boats from a bayside location ideal for dive trips to Sombrero Key. Some have fish finders, live wells and Bimini tops. They also rent all sorts of fishing equipment such as outriggers and gaffs, as well as diving gear. *Info: MM 47.5 BS, Marathon. Tel. 305-743-4403.*

Quality Boat Rentals

All of Quality's boats are set up for fishing and diving. They start at 20 feet and go up to 34 feet. Some are large enough to sleep on. Live wells, GPS and fish finders are standard. *Info: Marathon.*

www.qualityboats.net; Tel. 305-743-2895.

ATTRACTIONS

Most of the Keys have been spared the blight of gaudy tourist attractions. The Middle Keys fortunately, have few. Here are a few of the more obvious ones:

Dolphin Research Center

They like to term their dolphins "residents" rather than prisoners. Punters pay dearly to spend a few scant minutes in the water with a couple of captive dolphins. As with most dolphin exploitation attractions, kids pay full fare and must be accompanied by an adult, who also pays full fare. Things are situated so that it is hard for anyone but the Center's photographer to get decent pictures. Don't worry though - they'll sell you a CD with his shots on it for a mere $60.

Serious aquatic mammal researchers agree that if an organization is charging the public money to get in the water with their "research subjects," they are not a legitimate research organization. All the people I talk to enjoy their experience here,

although a few express some qualms about keeping such intelligent creatures in captivity (and profiting from it). *Info: Grassy Key, MM 59. www.dolphins.org; Tel. 305-289-0009.*

The Turtle Hospital

At the Turtle Hospital, injured sea turtles are lovingly rehabilitated, to be released back to the wild. Although turtles might not seem to be particularly interesting, the **90-minute tours** are actually quite informative and entertaining. You get to meet the turtles and observe therapy sessions. Call ahead, because they are sometimes booked up for weeks in advance. Skip the exploitive dolphin encounters and encounter a sea

SPORTS & RECREATION

turtle instead. At least these guys' intentions are to help the turtles get back to a free life in the sea. *Info: Marathon. www.turtlehospital.org; Tel. 305-743-2552.*

GOLF
Visitors to Marathon can select from two courses. Neither are spectacular but, for the addicted, playing them will probably get rid of your shakes for a day or two.

Key Colony Beach Golf & Tennis
Nine holer, par three. *Info: Key Colony Beach. Tel. 305-289-1533.*

Sombrero Country Club
A full 18-hole course. *Info: Marathon. Tel. 305-743-3433.*

BIRDING
As you approach Marathon in the winter, you should be

looking for the **magnificent frigate bird** *(photo below)* and short-tailed hawk. Summertime twitchers should look for the Antillean nighthawk around the Marathon airport, just before sunset. It's a bit smaller than the common nighthawk. The Antillean variety is known for its distinctive "pity, pit, pit" call. Fascinating. Burrowing owls nest on the golf course.

BEACHES, PARKS & ECO-WALKS
You can easily appreciate the beauty of the water and sea life around the Keys by taking a short walk on any of the old abandoned bridges left over from the Flagler railroad. The old **Seven Mile Bridge** is particularly good for a nature stroll. Bring a hat and sunscreen.

Pigeon Key
The little island you can see on the right as you cross the Seven Mile Bridge heading west is Pigeon Key. It was used as a construction camp and supply depot during construction of the railroad. It now houses a marine biology research station. If you would like to have a look, you can catch a shuttle out to the key

from the Marathon end of the bridge right by the Seven Mile Grille. It's good for a walk.

KAYAKING

The shallow, calm water with channels meandering through mangroves and turtle grass flats makes the Keys perfect kayaking territory. There are hundreds of sites where you can easily plop in a couple of kayaks and, moments later, find yourself deep in the wilderness. Kayaking through the mangroves and over the turtle grass flats is one eco-tour all visitors to the Keys should appreciate. This is a good way to get an up-close look at bird nesting sites, sharks, stingrays, sea urchins, crabs, Florida lobsters and all manner of blowfish and other strange critters.

The very best time to enjoy a quiet paddle on the flats is at daybreak or just before dark. This is when a lot of fishy activity begins. It's feeding time for some of the big boys like snapper, grouper, bonefish, sharks and permit. Drifting and paddling slowly around the miles and miles of turtle grass flats is a wonderful experience.

The currents can be quite strong, especially near bridges and in the channels between small keys or sand banks. If you time things right, you can plan your kayak trips to straddle a change in the tides. You can drift out on the last of the outgoing tide, and drift back in when the tide changes and starts to come back in. Try to plan your trips so you drift with the tide instead of fighting against it.

Any trips you make outdoors in the Keys require sunscreen, a hat and drinking water (beer, although also necessary, doesn't count). On a kayak or boat you are soaking up even more sun than usual, because the reflection from the water almost doubles your exposure to the effects of the sun.

Both **Booth Key** and **Cocoplum Beach** are good kayaking spots. You can park

and launch easily, and enjoy meandering through back passages in the mangroves and along the shallow reefs just offshore. For a really great paddle, launch at Sombrero Beach, find your way through the mangroves to the ocean side, then paddle along the shore to Cocoplum Beach. You can also cover much of this territory through the mangrove channels. Get a chart so you don't get lost.

Lots of places rent kayaks or lead kayak tours. Many lodges offer them to guests for free. These guys are about the best:

Marathon Kayak
Marathon can set you up with everything you need for an afternoon or overnight paddle. Most of their kayaks are the easy-to-use sit-on type. You can get **lessons** and go on **guided tours** with these guys. *Info: MM 50 OS, Sombrero Resort. www.marathonkayak.com: Tel. 305-395-0355.*

5. THE LOWER KEYS

HIGHLIGHTS

▲ Walking the old bridges and deserted beaches

▲ Kayak tour through the mangroves

▲ Diving and snorkeling Looe Key

▲ Fishing for snapper and hard-fighting billfish

▲ Cold beer, blues, and seafood in a basket

INTRO

The Lower Keys are very quiet. There doesn't seem to be a whole lot going on. On the surface, there doesn't seem to be much of anything to do. *Don't let this fool you!* Of course there are a couple of tropical watering holes that might warrant your attention for the best part of a day, but the most enjoyable things about the Lower Keys involve the water. The most magnificent reefs in the US are right here.

COORDINATES

The Lower Keys run from the end of the Seven Mile Bridge **MM 68 to Stock Island MM 6**. Big Pine Key is the largest of the **Lower Keys**. It's about a three-hour drive from Miami and a half hour from Key West. **Great Heron National Wildlife Refuge** borders the bay side and **the Florida Keys National Marine Sanctuary** protects the offshore reefs.

Fishing is superb both close to shore and offshore in the Gulf Stream. Diving and snorkeling are brilliant, especially at **Looe Key**. There are hundreds of small, very small, and even smaller bird-filled keys in this area. You simply must find a way onto some sort of boat, and float around the mangroves and turtle grass flats in Florida Bay. This is probably the best kayaking area in the Keys.

The Lower Keys is also home to the toniest lodging in the Keys. The $1,000-a-night resort called **Little Palm Island** is on **Little Torch Key**, and is accessible for guests by an elegant, handcrafted wooden launch.

Check into the wonderful, quiet **Little Palm Island Resort**. Spend most of your days out on the water: **dive**, **fish**, and **kayak through the mangroves**. In the evenings, indulge yourself shamelessly in seafood and umbrella drink consumption. Let them pamper you with five-star luxuries. Get your credit cards ready.

THE LOWER KEYS IN A DAY

The Lower Keys are a bit far from Miami for a day trip, but if you're staying in Key West for a few days it might be a good idea to get out of town for a day and enjoy the very laid-back atmosphere of **Big Pine Key** or **Geiger Key**. The Lower Keys are only a short ride from Key West.

SIGHTS

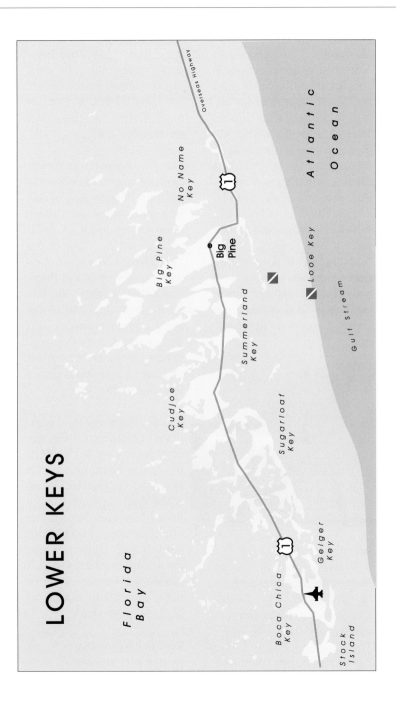

LOWER KEYS

Florida
Bay

Overseas Highway

No Name
Key

Big Pine
Key

Big
Pine

Cudjoe
Key

Summerland
Key

Sugarloaf
Key

Looe Key

Atlantic

Ocean

Gulf Stream

Boca Chica
Key

Geiger
Key

Stock
Island

SIGHTS

Morning

Not far out of Key West, you'll pass **Baby's** on the ocean side. Be sure to stop here for the full-on coffee experience. They roast their own beans, so the coffee is always delicious. After the quick coffee break, I would plan on spending the morning poking around the back sides of **Big Pine Key** or **Sugarloaf** (*photo below*) and driving around **No Name Key** looking for **Key deer**. Although seeing one is a thrill, they are just rather small deer so don't bust out crying if you don't get to see one.

Afternoon

A leisurely lunch at the **No Name Pub** (pizza and burgers) or, even better, at the **Geiger Key Smokehouse** (seafood in a basket and such) is in order. The No Name Pub is a little hard to find, but worth the look. They have cold beer, pizza, and dollar bills stuck on the walls all over the place. See *Best Sleeps & Eats* for more details on these and other restaurants.

Don't overdo it on lunch, because an afternoon dive just offshore at **Looe Key** is one adventure not to be missed. Looe Key is about six miles offshore at the edge of the **Gulf Stream**. There is not really any key or island there, but rather a large, shallow sandy area atop one of the most complex tongue and groove reef systems I've seen. When the water is calm the snorkeling and scuba diving here is superb.

It's easy to get in a solid afternoon or morning fishing. Anglers have a lot of choice in the Lower Keys. One of the best places to hunt for billfish is **The Wall** - - a "hump" in the floor of the Gulf Stream that concentrates swarms of baitfish into huge schools, attracting predators of all sizes. Big-time anglers fish for **tuna, swordfish, marlin** or perhaps **mako shark**.

Reef fishing for snapper, yellowtail and grouper is wonderful in this area, but there are relatively few boats that go out for this type of fishing. That's the advantage to the Lower Keys – it's not as crowded.

Flats fishing for bones, permit, shark, or perhaps a redfish is all the rage on the Gulf side. Fortunately there are few people out there raging after these fish, so you are likely to have a pleasant, quiet day fishing around the thousands of small mangrove keys.

There are always zillions of **barracuda** hanging around the shallower areas of the **Looe Key** reef system and you can easily hook them for **spectacular angling battles**. I always release the 'cudas I catch.

I suggest a period of time spent relaxing with beer after the day of exploring and diving or fishing.

Evening
For hanging around, beverage consumption, seafood baskets and blues you just can't beat the **Geiger Key Smokehouse**. It's not much more than a tiki bar at a marina but the atmosphere is great. There's a big old waterdog that hangs around and from time to time jumps in the water chasing after pelicans. This always gets a big laugh from the old soaks like me hanging around at the bar. They have live bands on the weekends and some weeknights. You can't miss this one. This is one of my favorite haunts.

As usual, one person in your group should remain stone cold sober to drive everyone home after having so much fun at the Geiger Key Smokehouse. You'll be back in Key West in less than an hour, perhaps ready to party some more.

SIGHTS

A WEEKEND IN THE LOWER KEYS

A weekend will give you time enough to sample the **wonderful fishing and diving** in the Lower Keys area. In my opinion, this is one of the best areas in the country to do both. You'll also have enough time to explore the scruffy back side of **Big Pine Key** by car, looking for the elusive **Key Deer**, and perhaps get out into **Florida Bay** by kayak. This also gives enough time to thoroughly enjoy one of the very best watering holes in the Keys: the **Geiger Key Smokehouse**.

Friday Evening

The important thing on the first day is to get out of the airport and/or Miami as quickly as possible. You can lose several hours in Miami traffic if you take the wrong route. See *Practical Matters* for the best route out of town.

The only road through the Keys is US 1, the famous **Overseas Highway**. Hurrying on the Overseas Highway is rarely possible and never a good idea. Radar traps are common.

Stop for lunch in Marathon at **Castaway's.** It is perhaps a little hard to find, but if you turn to the ocean side at MM 47.8 and follow your nose to the commercial fishing docks, you'll find it. This is not a fancy place at all, but the seafood is fresh and plentiful, and the beer is cold. It's one of my favorite eateries in the Keys.

When you arrive in the Lower Keys, you're either going to have to stay at one of the crummy budget dive motels or at the international, five-star-quality **Little Palm Island Resort** (*photo below*). There is not really any other choice. There are few places to stay in the relatively undeveloped Lower Keys.

If you choose the luxury route, the resort can make all arrangements for your fishing and diving adventures over the next two days. Hard-core divers want to spend their money on diving and beer instead of luxury lodgings, so they tend to concentrate at **Parmer's** and the salubrious **Looe Key Reef Resort**. See *Best Sleeps & Eats* for more details on these and other resorts and hotels.

The dining room at the **Little Palm Island Resort** will feed you memorable, exquisite cuisine but so will the funky, marina-side tiki bar, the **Geiger Key Smokehouse**. If you go for huge, juicy fish sandwiches and cold beer in a plastic cup served with live blues, this is the only choice.

Saturday

My suggestion is to sleep late Saturday morning, having a leisurely breakfast including mimosas, and then piddle around the resort checking out the amenities. In the afternoon the staff can arrange for a diving trip to nearby **Looe Key** or a sport fishing trip for sails, wahoo or dorado. Delicious umbrella drinks will await you when you get back from a hot afternoon on the water. I would definitely make early reservations for dinner in the world famous **Little Palm Island dining room**.

Of course, the main reason to hang around in this area is to enjoy the delights of the surrounding coral reefs and sand flats. **Looe Key** offers a relatively shallow, classic tongue and groove reef system leading from a shallow sandy shoal through twisting, sand-bottomed channels winding through the coral to the plunging blue of the **Gulf Stream**. It's one of the best dives in the Keys, and is good for beginners or snorkelers when the sea is calm.

Looe Key is not really a "key" or island at all. The reef gets quite shallow in places but there are no rocks or anything else above sea level. Reefs fringe the seaward side of a large, shallow sandy area which is itself surrounded by miles turtle grass and sand. The Gulf Stream lurks just a couple of hundred yards out. It is so close you can hear the underwater sounds of huge freighters chugging along in the shipping channel.

SIGHTS

ALTERNATE PLAN

Lounge around the pool all day Saturday enjoying refreshing tropical beverages. A couple of half-hour snorkel excursions in the shallow water in front of the resort can be followed by more pool time. Venture out in the evening to gorge on seafood and enjoy the sounds at one of the best bars in south Florida: **Geiger Key Smokehouse**. On Sunday take a short nature walk on the near end of the famous **Seven Mile Bridge** and head back to Miami with a pause for a nice seafood lunch at Ballyhoo's in Islamorada on the way back.

It's easy to get in a solid afternoon or morning fishing. Anglers have a lot of choice in the Lower Keys. One of the best places to hunt for billfish is **The Wall** – a "hump" in the floor of the Gulf Stream that concentrates swarms of baitfish into huge schools attracting predators of all sizes. Big-time anglers fish for **tuna, swordfish, marlin** or perhaps **mako sharks**.

Reef fishing for snapper, yellowtail and grouper is wonderful in this area, but there are relatively few boats that go out for this type of fishing.

That's the advantage to the Lower Keys — it's not as crowded.

Flats fishing for bones, permit, shark, or perhaps redfish is all the rage on the bay side. Fortunately there are few people out there raging after these fish so you are likely to have a pleasant, quiet day fishing around the thousands of small mangrove keys.

There are always zillions of **barracuda** hanging around the shallower areas of the **Looe Key** reef system and you can easily hook them for **spectacular angling battles**. I always release the 'cudas I catch.

There are many reliable charter captains and flats guides in the area.

If you just want to kick around on the cheap and fish a couple of good spots, I like to fish in the area at the west end of the new Bahía Honda Bridge. There is a lot of structure, and currents under the bridge funnel a huge amount of water back and forth between Florida Bay and the reefs.

The area around **Little Palm**

Island Resort is wonderful for **kayaking**. The water is calm almost all the time, and there has been little other development in the area. You can paddle out to some **shallow patch reefs** right in front of the resort and then follow the shoreline around to a small channel where you can cut through to the back side of the key and back to your luxury resort for a swim and a massage. Can't beat that!

Sunday

On Sunday morning wander around the back parts of **Summerland**, **Big Pine Key** and **No Name Key** looking for Key deer (*photo above at right*) and pirates. Stop in for a cold beer and some pizza in the dark, gloomy and interesting **No Name Pub**, popular with locals and tourists.

My idea of a great afternoon or evening out with my family and pals is enjoying a **seafood basket**, **cold beer** and **blues** in a tiki bar by a marina. I like to spend long afternoons and evenings in this manner. The **Geiger Key Smokehouse** is one of the best places in the world to do this. The atmosphere is truly the essence of the Keys experience. The grouper sandwiches ooze juice. The live music rocks. The beer is cold.

A WEEK IN THE LOWER KEYS

A long week in the Lower Keys is a great way to get away from the city. A week gives you time enough to fish the flats, the reefs and offshore in the Gulf Stream. A couple of days spent scuba diving, snorkeling and kayaking through the remote parts of Florida Bay still leaves plenty of time for poolside enjoyment of tropical adult beverages. You might even have enough time to sneak into Key West for a little wild partying or quiet sightseeing.

SIGHTS

Day One

The drive down is short enough to get you into your hotel around sunset if you leave Miami before noon on Friday. You'll have plenty of time for a wonderful seafood dinner followed by rockin' the night away to blues at the **Geiger Key Smoke House**.

If you get hungry along the way, stop at either the notorious **Alabama Jack's** just before the bridge into Key Largo, or **Denny's Latin Café** in a small shopping center on US 1 (serving the best cup of coffee in the Keys).

Days Two – Six

I suggest a more or less leisurely morning, perhaps by the pool or snorkeling close to wherever you are staying. Take stock of the area and perhaps drive around a little looking for Key deer.

Dining in the area is based around **fresh local seafood** and is fairly straightforward. If you are staying at Little Palm Island expect some of the best meals of your life.

Baby's Coffee Bar is good for a quick stop to caffeinate yourself. They have great fancy coffee to drink on the spot or to go. You can buy beans and various coffee-related gift things. **Sugarloaf Food Co.** is open for breakfast and lunch; you just can't beat the wonderful pastries and baked goodies served up by proprietress Anne Rodamer.

As I've said before and will say again, the **Geiger Key Smokehouse** is the top entertainment and fine beverage venue in the Lower Keys. For luxury dining eat at the **Little Palm Island Resort & Spa**. Other good choices are **Mangrove Mama's** and **No Name Pub**. For more details, see *Best Sleeps & Eats* later in this chapter.

Scuba diving and snorkeling can be split up into separate half-day trips, so you don't have to spend too much time out in the sun.

Looe Key is one of the finest specimens of the tongue and groove reef structure in North America and offers several dives worth of interesting formations and crazy reef creatures. It's one of the best dives in the Keys and is **good for beginners** or snorkelers when the sea is calm.

Looe Key is not really a "key" or island. The reef gets quite shallow in places, but there are no rocks or anything else above sea level. The Gulf Stream is so close you can hear the underwater sounds of huge freighters chugging along in the shipping channel.

There is an area of **patch reef** about a half mile off from the Little Palm Island Resort. It is clearly marked with four large buoys. Great snorkeling.

Not far from Looe Key, in the direction of American Shoals, you can find the buoy marking the **wreck of the Adolphus Busch**—a very fine, fairly deep dive with lots of very big fish.

There's one spectacular wreck in this area that's only for advanced divers. The *USS Wilkes-Barre* lies intact, in fact almost pristine, in 340 feet of water. The huge wreck rises to 140 feet. It's really too deep to dive the hull, but the wreck's superstructure has attracted huge schools of baitfish, pelagics, Goliath groupers and the occasional sperm whale. This dive is for seriously experienced deep-water divers only.

Even though there are not very many tourists in the area, there are plenty of charter boats

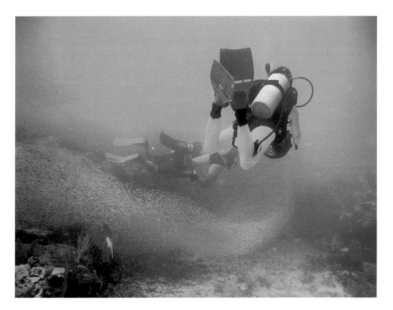

SIGHTS

and flats guides. It's easy to get in a solid afternoon or morning fishing. Anglers have a lot of choice in the Lower Keys.

One of the best places to hunt for billfish is **The Wall** — a "hump" in the floor of the Gulf Stream that concentrates swarms of baitfish into huge schools, attracting predators of all sizes. Big-time anglers fish for **tuna, swordfish, marlin** or perhaps **mako sharks**.

Reef fishing for snapper, yellowtail and grouper is wonderful in this area, but there are relatively few boats that go out for this type of fishing. That's the advantage to the Lower Keys—it's not as crowded.

Flats fishing for bones, permit, shark, or perhaps redfish is all the rage in the Gulf side. Fortunately, there are few people out there raging after these fish so you are likely to have a pleasant, quiet day fishing around the thousands of small mangrove keys.

There are always zillions of **barracuda** hanging around the shallower areas of the **Looe Key** reef system and you

can easily hook them for **spectacular angling battles**. I always release the 'cudas I catch.

There are many reliable charter captains and flats guides in the area.

If you just want to kick around on the cheap and fish a couple of good spots, I suggest the area at the west end of the new **Bahía Honda Bridge**. There is a lot of structure, and the currents under the bridge funnel a huge amount of water back and forth between Florida Bay and the reefs, bringing all sorts of interesting fishy things floating by.

If you drive all the way through **Sugarloaf Shores**, and turn right at the end of the road, you'll pass through some scruffy-looking areas, but eventually you'll get to a small bridge over a canal that separates an interior lagoon from the ocean. This is one of my secret fishing holes. You can occasionally land decent snapper here if you can keep them away from the 'cudas. From time to time tarpon come sliding through, usually hugging the sides of the canal. I like to have a couple of frisky pinfish in the water waiting for them.

The area around **Little Palm Island Resort** is wonderful for **kayaking**. The water is calm almost all of the time, and there has been little other development in the area. You can paddle out to some **shallow patch reefs** right in front of the resort, then follow the shoreline around to a small channel where you can cut through to the back side of the key and back to your luxury resort for a swim and a massage. Can't beat that!

Birders and wildlife lovers will enjoy poking around Big Pine and No Name Keys looking for the tiny **Key deer** or the elusive **mangrove cuckoo**.

You can do it without getting out of your car. The best way to watch birds in the Keys is from a kayak. This is a superb area for it. The shallow flats near the bridges close to Key West are havens for wading birds. Scrub on the ocean side of Summerland Key holds its own assortment of vireos, warblers and more common LBBs (Little Brown Birds).

Don't fail to take a trip to **Bahía Honda State Park**. It's definitely worth at least one visit. There is quite a long beach on the ocean side where you can easily spend a couple of hours examining the interesting things that wash up, and watching the terns, gulls and herons. Snorkeling and wading at this beach are great. At places, you can wade out on the flats for tremendous distances at low tide.

The whole park teems with birds, raccoons and weird crabs. The waters around it are full of fish. There is good beginner snorkeling in the protected swimming area near the main park buildings.

A walk on the spectacular old **Bahía Honda Bridge** gives you

SIGHTS

SIGHTS

ALTERNATE PLAN

Rent a houseboat and cruise the remote backwaters of Florida Bay through the turtle grass, sand flats and mangrove islands of Everglades National Park. Outfitters can have you all ready to go with your houseboat warmed up, beer in the fridge and bait in the live well. Just hop in after the ride down from Miami and begin serious decompression.

great views over the flats to the edge of the Gulf Stream. You can see huge tarpon swimming through the channel under the bridge and watch container ships plowing along the shipping channel a few miles off shore.

In July, area boosters put on the world famous **Underwater Music Festival**. At this unusual event, the venue is underwater at magnificent Looe Key. Classical and popular music is broadcast underwater to "spectators" who flock to the area for this out-of-the-ordinary concert.

Nightlife in this area is paltry, with one outstanding exception. The **Geiger Key Smokehouse** is a great, casual place to indulge in adult beverages and listen to blues. Sometimes the music is live. The conch fritters are always fresh.

Don't forget, the fleshy delights of Key West are only a short drive away. Partying to suit all tastes is close at hand. Be careful driving back at night, as police sobriety checkpoints are frequent.

Last Day

It's a pretty long haul back to Miami, but you don't have to worry about that until noon. Laze around the pool and take it easy for a couple of hours.

On the way back to Miami, I suggest stopping at all of the hot spots once again like **Denny's Latin Café** in Key Largo for a kick-ass cup of Cuban Coffee. Be sure to stop and have lunch or dinner at the **Whale Harbor Inn**. The enormous seafood buffet is

world famous. They have shrimp, crab, squid, prime rib, and the entire usual buffet stuff, but top quality and more of it. We always stopped here for dinner when I was a kid.

I usually take the Card Sound Road route back to the main-land, so I can stop at **Alabama Jack's** for one last taste of the Keys. Keep someone sober for the drive back. There are long stretches of two-lane highway. Nighttime driving here can be monotonous. Avoid head-on collisions.

BEST SLEEPS & EATS

BEST OF THE BEST IN THE LOWER KEYS
Little Palm Island $$$$$
A true luxury resort with a well-earned reputation, Little Palm Island begins to impress before you even arrive. The resort is actually on an isolated island that cannot be reached by car. Guests are met at a landing and are discretely ushered onto a wooden launch like something from *On Golden Pond*.

Facilities and grounds are immaculate and tropically lush. There are plenty of private nooks and crannies set up with hammocks and terrycloth-covered chaise lounges. The whole place is as quiet as a library (no cell phones allowed except in your room). The service is also quiet and efficient. Very romantic.

Rooms are isolated and quiet. Mattresses and all the trimmings are top quality. Bathroom goodies are organic and profuse. The use of some of the goos and ointments involving oatmeal is obscure. The spa includes exotic body treatments, Indonesian and Thai rituals, massage therapy, and an extensive fitness center. Healing and meditation classes are offered. They have a small sandy beach, pool and marina. There is unquestionably

SLEEPS & EATS

the best diving and fishing in the Keys directly offshore. Good patch reefs are within kayaking distance. The resort arranges everything for all these activities or will rent you a small Whaler and point you in the right direction.

Do not miss guzzling one of their signature cocktails: the Gumby Slumber. They've got a lot of rum in them and my experience is you get kind of gummed up then go on to slumber in a hammock. This is a good thing. *Info: MM 28.5 OS, Little Torch Key. www.littlepalmisland.com; Tel. 305-872-2524.*

Looe Key Reef Resort & Dive Center $$

The lodging is basic, motel-style in need of maintenance but there are few choices in the area. The dive operation is also in need of maintenance. There is a boat ramp, small pool and marina. *Info: MM 27.5 OS, Ramrod Key. www.diveflakeys.com; Tel. 305-872-2215.*

Parmer's Resort $$$

Parmer's has an 'Old Keys' atmosphere. They have a pool, ramp and dock and spacious grounds. Most of the rooms are motel-style but there also some efficiencies and multi-bedroom suites. They throw in a nice breakfast. This is one of the very best choices in the area. *Info: MM 28.5 BS, Little Torch Key. www.parmersplace.com; Tel. 305-872-2157.*

Sugarloaf Lodge $$

The motel suffered extensive hurricane damage but they seem to have recovered. It is still a little shabby but OK for one night or two if you can't get into Parmer's. Some cute touches from the 50s, like bedsteads with built-in radios (non-functional), remain. The views from most rooms are good and there is a marina next door. The restaurant is dire. The tiki bar is great with live music some nights. *Info: MM 17 BS, Summerland Key. www.sugarloaflodge.net; Tel. 800-553-6097, 305-745-3211.*

There are not very many choices for eating out in the Lower Keys but a couple of those few places are great. Perhaps the best place in South Florida to honk down seafood, drink beer, listen to live blues music, and generally go to seed is the **Geiger Key Smoke House** on Geiger Key. Without doubt, the finest top end dining in the Keys occurs at the dining room at the **Little Palm Island Resort**. There are a couple of other OK places to eat but really, you don't need much more than these two.

Baby's Coffee Bar $$
This is good for a quick stop to caffeinate yourself for the drive back to Miami, or any other reason. They have great fancy coffee to drink on the spot or to go. You can buy beans and various coffee-related gift things. *Info: MM 15 OS. Tel. 305-744-9866.*

Geiger Key Smokehouse $$
The top entertainment and fine beverage venue in the Lower Keys is without a doubt the **Geiger Key Smokehouse**. This is a in

simple place—not much more than a tiki bar at a marina. The atmosphere is quite laid-back since you're basically hanging out at a simple tiki bar at a marina. The beer is cold and is served in plastic cups. Their food is a wonderful example of the best seafood basket-type cuisine. Fish sandwiches ooze juice. Mounds of French fries, crab cakes, shrimp, and cold beer entice diners. Blues is the preferred music, with live bands most weekends and sometimes during the week.

If you go for huge, juicy fish sandwiches and cold beer in a plastic cup served with live blues, Geiger Key Smokehouse is the only choice. They feature local and national entertainers Friday through Sunday (it's an early evening sort of place - the music's over at 9pm). There's a big old waterdog that hangs around and from time to time jumps in the water chasing after pelicans. This always gets a big laugh from the old soaks like me at the bar.

SLEEPS & EATS

SLEEPS & EATS

This is one of my favorite hangouts. *Info: MM 10.5, Geiger Key. www.geigerkeymarina.com, Tel. 305-296-3553.*

The Dining Room, Little Palm Island Resort & Spa $$$$

The food in the Dining Room is termed "modern tropical cuisine," and aficionados come from as far as Miami for tables

reserved far in advance. Executive Chef Louis Pous and his culinary team prepare the ultimate seaside dining experience. "A vibrant blend of French and Pan Latin flavors." They'll set up a secluded table for you with linen and crystal on the beach in the moonlight or anywhere on the resort grounds. Very romantic. The wine list is sophisticated (not cheap) and received an Award of Excellence from the *Wine Spectator* in 2006. They have a very good selection of wines by the glass, including a couple of interesting rosés. Spanish wines, trendy stars in the wine world recently, are only adequately represented however. Foodies rate this one of the very best restaurants in Florida. Sunday brunch is imposing and decadent. *Info: MM 28.5 OS, Little Torch Key. www.littlepalmisland.com; Tel. 305-872-2551.*

Mangrove Mama's $$

Black and blue fish sandwich? Wonderful! This strange concoction involves a blackened fish with blue cheese dripping with wonderful juice out of a bun. Mama's is a relaxed, Keys-type place with both inside and outside seating. Try the conch fritters. Buffalo conch is another of their unique suggestions. *Info: MM 20 BS, Sugarloaf Key. www.mangrovemamasrestaurant.com, Tel. 305-745-3030.*

No Name Pub $$

This place is a little hard to find, but perhaps the challenge of the hunt is part of the attraction. Other than that, I'm not sure why every tourist seems to want to find the place, have a beer, and buy the T-shirt. The food is okay (pizza, burgers), the atmosphere is rather gloomy, and the walls are covered with dollar bills and other typical bar décor. Key deer are thick in the area, so you could just drive on past, see some tiny deer and then

head over to the Geiger Key Smokehouse for some seafood. *Info: MM 31 BS, North Watson Boulevard, Big Pine Key. www.nonamepub.com, Tel. 305-872-9115.*

Sugarloaf Food Co. $$

You just can't beat the wonderful pastries and baked goodies served up by proprietress Anne Rodamer. This spot is open for breakfast and lunch, and they tend to have interesting vegetarian specials. *Info: MM 24.5 BS, Summerland Key. www.sugar loaffood.com, Tel. 305-744-0631.*

CONCH FRITTERS

Conch (pronounced "conk") fritters are made from the critters that live inside those huge shells you see guys wearing grass skirts blowing into at tourist shows. Conch itself is fairly tasteless and chewy but if you bread it with spicy, salty glop and deep-fry it you have conch fritters. Tourists love 'em. If not prepared properly, conch can be rubbery and tasteless, but you have about an even chance of getting a good fritter here in the Keys. A good fritter is served piping hot, the interior is soft, and the conch is chewable.

SHOPPING

BEST SHOPPING

The Lower Keys have no shell shops and not much in the way of painted driftwood or T-shirts either. Oh, well. Key West is not far away, and is thick with these types of shopping opportunities. Here are two recommendations:

Key Collections
Features tropical resort clothing. *Info: Big Pine Key. Tel. 305-872-4491.*

Artists in Paradise Gallery
A collective outlet for over 30 Lower Keys artists. They have consigned stained glass, watercolors, ceramics, jewelry, sculpture, feather art and more. *Info: Big Pine Key. www.theartistsinparadise.com; Tel. 305-872-1828.*

NIGHTLIFE & ENTERTAINMENT

BEST NIGHTLIFE & ENTERTAINMENT

The Lower Keys are not noted for wild partying, or even for much partying at all, but there a few good possibilities for stirring things up.

Geiger Key Smokehouse
This is without a doubt the top entertainment and fine beverage venue in the Lower Keys the Geiger Key Smokehouse. It's a simple place with a laid-back atmosphere—not much more than a tiki bar at a marina. The beer is cold and is served in plastic cups. Their food is a wonderful example of the best seafood basket-type cuisine. Fish sandwiches ooze juice. Mounds of French fries, crab cakes, shrimp, and cold beer

entice diners. Steaks on Saturday and BBQ on Sunday. What a deal! Blues is the preferred music with live bands most weekends and sometimes during the week. This is one of my favorite hangouts. Not to be missed. *Info: Geiger Key. www.geigerkeymarina.com; Tel. 305-296-3553.*

House of Music
An oasis of good sounds, beer and fun. Owned and operated by musician Angus Brangus (no kidding), this place has your basic bar food and beer along with the usual karaoke, open mike nights and live music on the weekends. *Info: MM31, Big Pine Key. Tel. 305-872-9000.*

Looe Key Tiki Bar
This is your regular old tiki bar at a rundown resort. The drinks are okay. It's big enough that you can make a small party off to yourself and not have to interact with a lot of bozos. *Info: MM 27.5 OS, Ramrod Key at the Looe Key Resort. Tel. 305-872-2215.*

BEST SPORTS & RECREATION

DIVING & SNORKELING
Looe Key is the big attraction for divers and snorkelers in the Lower Keys. It is a very colorful reef system with plenty of shallow areas and some interesting deep ball formations a little farther out. Looe Key offers a relatively shallow classic tongue and groove reef system leading from a shallow sandy shoal through twisting, sand-bottomed channels winding through the coral to the plunging blue of the **Gulf Stream**. It's one of the best dives in the Keys, and is good for beginners or snorkelers when the sea is calm.

Looe Key is not really a "key" or island at all. The reef gets quite shallow in places, but there are no rocks or anything else above sea level. Reefs fringe the seaward side of a large, shallow sandy area, which is itself surrounded by miles of turtle grass and sand.

This area is **chock full of barracuda**. The Gulf Stream lurks flows just a couple of hundred yards out. It is so close that you can hear the underwater sounds of huge freighters chugging along in the shipping channel.

There are some areas of **patch reef** about a half mile off from the Little Palm Island Resort. They are clearly marked with four large buoys. Great snorkeling.

Not far from Looe Key, in the direction of American Shoals, you can find the buoy marking the wreck of the *Adolphus*

SPORTS & RECREATION

Busch—a very fine, fairly deep dive with lots of very big fish.

There's one spectacular wreck in this area that's only for advanced divers. The *USS Wilkes-Barre* lies intact, in fact almost pristine, in 340 feet of water. The huge wreck rises to 140 feet. It's really too deep to dive the hull, but the wreck's superstructure has attracted huge schools of baitfish, pelagics, Goliath groupers and the occasional sperm whale. This dive is for seriously experienced deep-water divers only.

Here are my favorite operators in the Lower Keys:

Innerspace Diving & Snorkeling Center
Well situated to access Looe Key and American Shoals, Innerspace offers dives with six or fewer divers per boat. Nitrox, PADI, NAUI. *Info: MM 29.5 OS, Big Pine Key. www.diveinnerspace.com; Tel. 305-872-2319.*

Looe Key Reef Resort & Dive Center
Cattle boat with up to 45 "divers." *Info: www.diveflakeys.com; Tel. 305-872-4244.*

Paradise Divers Inc.
Six-packs and larger boats. *Info: MM 38.5 BS. Tel. 305-872-1114.*

Underseas, Inc.
Big Pine cattle operation with one 45-person pontoon boat that makes trips to Looe Key and the Adolphus Busch. PADI training is available. *Info: Big Pine Key, MM 30.5. Tel. 305-872-2700.*

DEEPER THAN THOU

Some divers, often relative newbies, seem to think dives must be deep, in caves or on wrecks to be good enough for them. They pride themselves on the danger quotient of the dives they talk about. Here's a hint from experienced divers: deep dives are shorter. You see fewer fish and other marine life on deep dives. Colors fade with depth, so deep dives are colorless. My favorite dives are in 30 feet or less. I get to stay down much longer and see many more fish and lots of colorful coral. Let the braggarts brag. The best dives are usually fairly shallow.

FISHING

There are several ways to enjoy fishing in the area. The easiest, and the most likely to end up with you catching fish, is to charter a boat for the day. Flats fishing for bonefish, tarpon and permit is usually done in a small skiff with two guests and the guide poling the boat around the sand and turtle grass flats. Trolling offshore for billfish will more likely find you coming home with dorado (mahi) and wahoo for dinner, but that's all right.

If you want to enjoy fishing and don't want to spend hundreds of dollars on a charter you can simply buy some shrimp and head to one of the abandoned Flagler railroad bridges and join the rest of the bridge fishing brigade. This is a nice way to spend a few hours (bring something to drink, a hat and sunscreen) out on the water. **Bridge fishing** may seem a little down market at first, but it is nothing to be ashamed of. It's fun, you might catch some fish and you have an excuse to piddle around the old bridges talking to old salts, fool around with your fishing tackle and poke at crabs.

The west end of the **Bahía Honda Bridge** is a good fishing spot. I've hauled in grouper, snapper, sharks, ladyfish and puffers, and thrown my bait at several tarpon. There is a good parking lot and some shade for the non-anglers.

If you drive all the way through **Sugarloaf Shores** and turn right at the end of the road, you pass through some scruffy looking areas, but eventually get to a small bridge over a canal that separates an interior lagoon from the ocean. This is one of my secret fishing holes. You can occasionally get decent snapper here if you can keep them away from the 'cudas. From time to time tarpon come sliding through, usually hugging the sides of the canal. I like to have a couple of frisky pinfish in the water waiting for them.

SPORTS & RECREATION

Several "humps" rise from the floor of the **Gulf Stream**, causing current upwellings that concentrate baitfish and attract game fish. Savvy charter captains punch the GPS coordinates of these humps into their autopilots and help guests hook up billfish, tuna or wahoo.

One of the humps off Big Pine is well known as a **swordfish** hole. Fishing for this delicious species is done at night with small chemical lights attached next to your hook to attract these big bruisers.

Anglers up north spend their Saturday mornings in the winter hunched over their TVs watching their favorite fishing stars haul in **snook**, **trout**, **bonefish**, **dorado** and other interesting game fish. Chances are the action they are watching is going on in the Keys. The Keys are one of North America's top fishing destinations, with three main types of angling action. **Bones**, **permit**, **tarpon** and other exotics school up around the flats and channels. **Huge snapper**, **grouper**, **yellowtail** and **kingfish** swarm around the reefs. **Marlin**, **amberjack** and **sails**

lurk just offshore in the Gulf Stream. Occasionally, **great white sharks** are hooked. The best tarpon months are April, May, and June. The bonefish are in the area year-round, but the best months are in the spring and fall.

There are many reliable charter captains and flats guides in the area. Here are some of my favorites:

Sea Boots Charters

Captain Jim Sharpe has been taking anglers out to some of the best fishing spots in the Keys for over 40 years. The guy knows what he's doing. He has a well-equipped 43-foot sport fisherman (*see photo on previous page*) with all the goodies. *Info: Summerland Key. www.seaboots.com; Tel. 305-745-1530.*

Helicon Backcountry Charters

Captain Michael Vaughn takes punters to the small mangrove islands and turtle grass flats of Florida Bay for tarpon, snook, trout and reds. He's got a great boat for it. *Info: Cudjoe Key. www.heliconfishing.com; Tel. 305-745-2800.*

BOATING

There is a wide variety of boat rental operators. Check their web sites and call in advance to be sure they have the type of boat and equipment you need. Be sure to reserve well in advance. Some rental operators will deliver the boat if you are renting for several days.

Renting a car while on vacation in an unfamiliar area is a great way to see the sights around you. Renting a boat in the Keys is much the same (as long as you know what you're doing). The best things about the Keys are in the water and you need a boat to get to them.

Some area boat rental operators don't want their boats in the shallows of Florida Bay, where you will almost certainly run aground and damage the prop if you don't know the waters very well. This is expensive for you, the renter, and a source of annoyance for the rental operator who will have to do the repairs. Other operators supply only a very short anchor line so you can't go out too far and anchor near the reefs. Some of them don't seem to want

you to actually use the boat for much of anything but putt-putting around very slowly. Others are well set up and ready to help you get the most out of your time on the water in their boats. Be sure to call ahead and find out what restrictions, if any, they impose. Find out in advance what type of equipment is available with the boats. You will want a diving ladder if you're snorkeling or scuba diving and a live well if you are fishing. Call ahead!

Keys Boat

Boat rentals for fishing, diving, snorkeling, swimming or just zooming around. They deliver with weekly rentals. *Info: Big Pine Key. www.keysboat.com; Tel. 305-664-2203.*

Dolphin Marina

These guys rent nice T-tops, but don't allow their boats to be used in Florida Bay. *Info: Little Torch Key, MM 28.5. www.dolphinmarina.net; Tel. 800-553-0308.*

Boating in the Keys is not like driving. There are no street signs or stop signs. Sand bars and reefs pop up unexpectedly. Damage to props on

SPORTS & RECREATION

rental boats is routine. There are extremely stiff fines for damaging coral or sand and grass flats with your boat or its propeller. The fines are calculated by the square inch of damage to the bottom. Damage to the bottom of your boat is a matter between you and the rental operator. Unless you know what you're doing, do your boating with guides, in their boats.

ATTRACTIONS
Roadside attractions in the Lower Keys, cheesy or otherwise, are just about non-existent. This is a good thing, as it keeps the hordes in Key West. There are however, a couple of sort-of interesting places to visit.

Bat Tower
The Bat Tower is a largish wooden structure built by a local visionary who hoped the tower would attract bats that would eat all the mosquitoes in the area, thus kicking off a tourism boom. No bats arrived, the skeeters still rule, no tourism boom exploded and the wooden structure remains supremely uninteresting. *Info: Sugarloaf Key, MM 17.*

Blue Hole

A small hole in the ground filled with clear water attracts the occasional gawker looking for alligators. Not worth the effort to find it. *Info: Key Deer Blvd, Big Pine Key.*

BIRDING
With over 200 species of birds available for your twitching pleasure, the Lower Keys are an often-overlooked paradise for birders. Bald eagles, reddish egrets, the elusive mangrove cuckoo, frigate birds, cormorants, anhingas, red-shouldered hawks, and, of course, roseate spoonbills abound. The shallow flats near the bridges close to Key West are havens for wading birds. Scrub on the ocean side of Summerland Key holds its own assortment of vireos, warblers and more common LBBs (Little Brown Birds).

BEACHES, PARKS & ECO-WALKS
You can easily appreciate the beauty of the water and sea life around the Keys by taking a short walk on any of the old abandoned bridges left over from the Flagler railroad. The old **Bahía Honda Bridge** is particularly good for a nature

stroll. Bring a hat and sunscreen.

Bahía Honda State Park
Definitely worth at least one visit even if you are just driving by on your way to Key West. There is quite a long beach on the ocean side where you can easily spend a couple of hours examining the interesting things that wash up, and watching the terns, gulls and herons.

When I was a kid I stopped here with my family one time and I immediately spied a small nurse shark in the shallows. I ran into the water and started dragging the thing around by the tail. My parents freaked, thinking I was bound to get a leg or arm bit off. Don't do what I did. It's bad mojo to bother the wildlife. Snorkeling and wading at this beach are great. At places, you can wade out on the flats for tremendous distances at low tide.

The whole park teems with birds, raccoons and weird crabs; the waters around it are full of fish. There is good beginner snorkeling in the protected swimming area near the main park buildings.

One of my favorite adventures in the park is to walk out on the old **Bahía Honda Bridge**. It's a spectacular old structure, and gives you great views from up high out over the flats to the edge of the Gulf Stream. You can see huge tarpon swimming through the channel under the bridge and watch container ships plowing along the shipping channel a few miles off shore.

When you're finished with the park, stop at the small parking area at the west end of the bridge, ocean side. This is a good place to get yet another good view of the remarkable old bridge. *Info: MM 37. Tel. 305-872-2353.*

FESTIVALS & PARTIES
An inspired, tourist-attracting gimmick, the **Underwater Music Festival** can be quite fun. Classical and popular music is broadcast underwa-

SPORTS & RECREATION

ter to hordes of scuba and snorkeling fans. All the local dive boats take punters out to Looe Key for the event. *Info: July, Big Pine Key. Tel. 305-872-2411.*

KAYAKING

The very best time to enjoy a quiet paddle on the flats is at daybreak or just before dark. This is when a lot of fishy activity begins. It's feeding time for some of the big boys like snapper, grouper, bonefish, sharks and permit. Drifting and paddling slowly around the miles and miles of turtle grass flats is a wonderful experience.

The shallow, calm water with channels meandering through mangroves and turtle grass flats makes the Keys perfect kayaking territory. There are hundreds of sites where you can easily plop in a couple of kayaks and, moments later,

find yourself deep in the wilderness. Kayaking through the mangroves and over the turtle grass flats is one eco-tour all visitors to the Keys should appreciate. This is a good way to get an up-close look at bird nesting sites, sharks, stingrays, sea urchins, crabs, Florida lobsters and all manner of blowfish and other strange critters.

There are some wonderful paddles through the shallow flats inside Sugarloaf and Saddlebunch Keys. The water is calm, but look out for strong currents near channels.

The currents can be quite strong, especially near bridges and in the channels between small keys or sand banks. If you time things right, you can plan your kayak trips to straddle a change in the tides. You can drift out on the last of the outgoing tide and drift back in when the tide changes and starts to come back in. Try to plan your trips so you drift with the tide instead of fighting against it.

Any trips you make outdoors in the Keys require sunscreen, a hat and drinking water (beer, although also necessary, doesn't count). On a kayak or boat you are soaking up even more sun than usual, because the reflection from the water almost doubles your exposure to the effects of the sun.

Sugarloaf Marina
Kayaks and canoes go for $15 an hour. They are nicely located to paddle off into the small mangrove keys and flats. *Info: MM17. Tel. 305-745-3135.*

Big Pine
Kayak Adventures
This is a very well equipped outfitter. They have all the latest types of kayaks, including sit-on fishing kayaks. They offer half- and full-day nature tours, eco-tours and short and long term kayak rentals. *Info: Big Pine Key. www.keyskayaktours.com; Tel. 305-872-7474.*

6. KEY WEST

HIGHLIGHTS

▲ Strolling Duval Street and Sunset Pier

▲ Sloppy Joe's bar featuring Pete and Wayne

▲ Fort Jefferson by seaplane

▲ Fishing for snapper and billfish

▲ Fabulous seafood

COORDINATES

Key West (pop. 25,000) is the largest city in the Keys. It's about a four-hour drive from Miami. To the west is **Fort Jefferson** in the **Dry Tortugas**. At the end of US 1, look for **MM 0**.

INTRO

Key West is one of North America's greatest party and tourist towns, combining quaint historic ambiance with a legendary tolerance for alternative lifestyles. Wonderful restaurants, great bars and clubs and an unbelievable street scene compete with bird watching, scuba diving, kayaking, and deep sea fishing. The "Conch Republic" is always warm and always open for fun.

The town of Key West is famous for being lifestyle-tolerant and gay-friendly. This attitude probably contributes to the wonderful air of controlled rebellion that permeates the many dedicated party events such as **Fantasy Fest, Hemingway Days, Conch Republic Days** or the **Poker Run**. The place is always jumpin'!

Many of the architecturally interesting old homes in the **Old Town** area have been restored to comfortable splendor and are continuing their lives as B&Bs and boutique hotels. They're great. If you can afford to stay in one of these beautiful old houses behind **Duval Street** you should splurge and do it. I'm particularly fond of the **Marquesa Hotel** on Fleming Street. A group of Old Town homes grouped around a pool have been renovated tastefully. It's a peaceful place yet close to the action.

Drive down from Miami and check into one of the wonderful, quiet Old Town boutique hotels. Go ahead and let yourself be a tourist in this wonderfully tacky tourist town. Make the scene on Duval Street. Sample the bars and crazy clubs. Spend your days recovering from the night before or out on the water: dive, fish, kayak through the mangroves and fly by seaplane to Fort Jefferson in the nearby Dry

Tortugas. In the evenings, indulge yourself shamelessly in seafood and umbrella drink consumption.

The food in Key West is great, with something for everyone. Funky Cuban cafes compete with fancy-shmancy drizzly-sauce fusion places serving seafood with the very latest of west coast/Pac rim/ mojo sauce smothered lima beans. Or whatever. There are a couple of wonderful hole-in-the-wall (literally) joints where steaming hot fresh seafood comes to you on waxed paper. Delicious! Try the fritters.

Key West Express, , has recently introduced a great new way to get to Key West from Miami. They offer four-hour trips via new, comfortable, high-speed catamaran for only $100 round trip. The boat leaves Miami at 8:30am from a dock next to the Seaquarium and arrives in Key West at 12:30pm. The return trip leaves at 5:30pm and gets into Miami at 9:30pm. This would be great for a weekend trip. You can't drive down from Miami that fast, and you don't need a car in Key West anyway. *Info: Tel. 866-593-3779.*

SIGHTS

KEY WEST IN A DAY 🚶

You can get a feel for what this wonderful tourist town has to offer quickly, and begin to have fun immediately. The town is small and you can get to almost all of the sights and attractions quickly on foot. There are literally dozens of tempting watering holes and places to eat with outdoor terraces so you can watch the passing parade of fellow weirdoes and fellow tourists.

Morning
I know it is extremely touristy, but it's hard to beat the Conch Train for getting a quick orientation tour around town and find out quickly what's of interest for you. The silly trains leave from Mallory Square and make a few stops at strategic points of interest. The **Old Towne Trolley** is perhaps a better option since

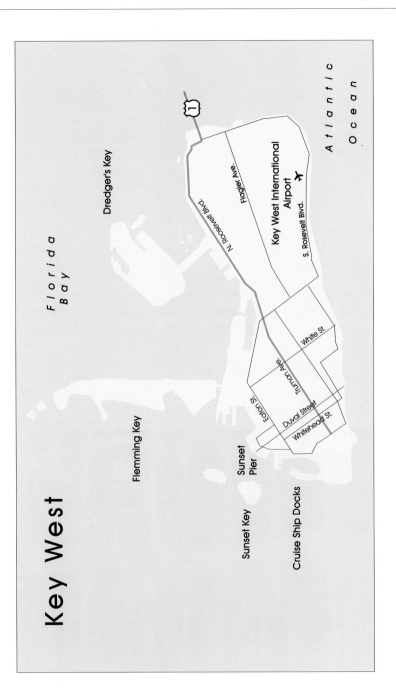

SIGHTS

it has more stops and your ticket lets you hop on and off all day.

You'll have plenty of time to stroll up and down **Duval Street** checking out the dubious shopping opportunities and trying to decide which cheesy tourist bars to visit.

It's easy to rent a bike or moped to zip around town, but be wary of the heavy traffic. Beware of drinking even mild alcoholic beverages while operating any sort of vehicle—even a bicycle. **Paradise Scooter Rentals** rents bikes and scooters. The scooters run around $25 an hour or $60 for all day. They have a booth at 430 Duval Street.

Lloyd's Original Key West Bike Tours is the most talked-about tour in Key West. Mr. Lloyd leads guided bike tours through the scenic back streets and popular tourist areas of Key West, specializing in keeping kids fascinated. He makes several stops to sample fresh fruit picked from trees along the route.

On the **Discovery Glass Bottom Boat** you can keep your feet dry and still experience spectacular coral gardens. The reefs off Key West are some of the most spectacular in the world and it would be a shame to miss them just because you can't get in the water for one reason or another. They offer three trips a day.

SIGHTS

The beautiful old **Harry S. Truman Little White House** is wonderfully maintained and loaded with historically significant items. The atmosphere is just like the old days. Guides schooled in the most trivial of Truman trivia lead informative tours. The tour I was on included a real Truman nerd who tried hard to stump the guide. Couldn't be done.

Ernest Hemingway Home & Museum (Whitehead Street) has an extra, odd attraction: cats with too many toes. The Hemingway cats have been inbreeding for so long they have little oddities (like too many toes) that endear them to the tourist public. The house is full of memorabilia. The 75 + cats are mostly in the garden. They are open every day of the year.

I've been coming to the **Key West Aquarium** since I was eight years old and I still love the place. It's very far from being a big-time, multi-media aquarium with albino sperm whales, but it is a good exhibit with its own Old Key West Charm. The shark cage out back is always a hoot.

Just visiting a few attractions

GETTING NAKED!

Everybody always wants to know if it's OK to go around naked in Key West. No. It's not. There are a few nude beaches (mentioned in the "Beaches" sections) and things can get a little weird on Duval Street during some of the rowdier festivals. At times, wearing nothing more than spray paint is not "naked." Just don't push it.

in the morning gets you up and down Duval Street without making a special effort to cruise the famous scene. Pick out a lunch spot that gives you a good view of the passing parade of tourists and bizarre spectacles.

The best thing about **Mangoes Restaurant & Catering** is the location right on Duval Street. It's hard to beat for people watching.

From time to time, the old guy living at 308 Petronia Street tacks a small menu on his door and begins selling his special: **Nasty Burgers**. That's all he sells. It's worth a visit to Key West just for a nasty burger. See *Best Sleeps & Eats* for information about

SIGHTS

these and other delightful places to eat in Key West.

Afternoon

Even with only one day in town, you have time to go out to the nearby, spectacular coral reefs for **snorkeling**, **scuba diving** or **fishing**. The sea around Key West has some of the finest and most pristine remaining coral reefs in North America. **Blue Water Charters** specializes in scuba, snorkeling and fishing trips to some of the more remote and obscure sites and can create custom trips for small groups.

A **kayaking** trip is not to be missed if you like the outdoors. Nearby **Florida Bay** and **Everglades National Park** have hundreds of square miles

WILD DOLPHIN ENCOUNTER

Swimming in the open ocean with truly wild dolphins is better than paying to swim with enslaved ones, and several places in the Keys offer such opportunities. My experience is that wild dolphins may cavort around a bit when snorkelers appear in the water with them, but they don't come close enough for you to rub them on the tummy.

ALTERNATE PLAN

Drink in the Duval Street bars all day and make the scene at Sunset Pier for sunset. Eat dinner somewhere and continue drinking in other Duval Street bars through the evening. Go back to your hotel. Pass out. Wake up in the morning. Repeat.

of turtle grass and sand flats dotted with small mangrove keys. **Lazy Dog Outfitters** rents all sorts of kayaks and fun watercraft. If you're into kayak fishing, this is the place.

If you are not the active outdoorsy type, you still have a big selection of activities for an afternoon of fun. Make a quick shopping trip down Duval Street to buy resort wear and gifts for the grandkids back home. Try **Summersalt** on Front Street for tank tops, Ts, sandals, bathing suits and all manner of tropical resort wear, or **Tropical Wave** on Duval. Yes, the tykes need Jimmy Buffett shirts too.

Beware of the loud T-shirt shops on Duval Street. Some will try a high-pressure bait and switch. You didn't really think they were going to have any decent T-shirts for $1, did you?

SIGHTS

County Beach on Atlantic Avenue (more or less at the far end of Duval Street) is loaded with public beach amenities like volleyball and food stands. There's not any surf to speak of but you can snorkel a little bit or just walk around soaking up the sun and sights.

Most visitors to Key West spend a significant part of their afternoons exploring the local, tourist-oriented drink emporiums. This is a good thing. It keeps them off the streets. Moving around town earlier in the day gives you a chance to select a couple of likely-looking spots for the enjoyment of tropical adult beverages, or beer. Duval Street has plenty. I suggest spending the last part of the afternoon sloshing around the **Schooner Wharf Bar** on William Street before the dinner crowd shows up and ruins everything.

Schooner Warf is convenient since you could just crawl from the bar to the next event: a sunset cruise on the **Schooner Appledore Champagne Sunset Sail**. Yes, it's a little touristy but you get to putt around the harbor a little and see the scene at Sunset Pier

from a somewhat different perspective (and a safe distance).

Evening
Well before you arrive in Key West you need to find out if the hilarious duo **Pete & Wayne** will be playing at **Sloppy Joes**. If they are, you have to plan your day around catching their act. It usually starts at 5:30, which may interfere slightly with any plans for watching the sun go down somewhere besides the inside of a bar (actually, you can watch the sun go down from inside several bars in Key West). You can catch the crazy action at **Sunset Pier** just a little bit later.

Key West features numerous wonderful restaurants, but you need to know where you're going to avoid the many overpriced tourist traps. Seafood is the best thing to

SIGHTS

look for. You'll need reservations for some of the more popular places like **Seven Fish** which features fresh, local fish in a variety of interesting sauces. Not a fancy place but great.

Another great spot for a popular meal is **Louie's Backyard**. Lots of atmosphere and wonderful conch fritters. Jimmy Buffett used to play here for tips and beer.

After dinner, the scene along Duval Street will be even wilder. If you select carefully, you may be able to snag a table overlooking the sidewalk so you can gawk and carry out more drinking. **Mangoes** is good for this but they'll want you to buy food—not just drink.

See *Best Sleeps & Eats* for information about these and other delightful places to eat in Key West.

Hard Rock, Margaritaville, Sloppy Joe's, Irish Kevin's, Hog's Breath, Captain Tony's and **Schooner Wharf** are perhaps the most popular drinking venues—tourists from Ardmore or Carbondale, just like yourself, will surround you. Sloppy Joe's is the best of the lot. They have honest drinks and good live entertainment.

Later in the evening, you need to swing by the **Green Parrot** (Whitehead Street) to see if they have a good band. This is a good, plain old music bar with plenty of locals hanging about playing pool. If you are feeling a little bit wilder, head to the **Garden of Eden** (Duval Street) upstairs in the Bull & Whistle for **nude cocktails and dancing** - just the thing to tell everybody about when you get back to Sioux City. What a way to end the day! See *Best Nightlife* for more information.

SIGHTS

🚶 A WEEKEND IN KEY WEST

Key West is the party time Emerald City at the end of the Yellow Brick Road. You can run around naked, get drunk, sing and shout until the wee hours of the morning. But partying isn't the only attraction. Key West is also one of the finest areas in the world for water sports and enjoying relatively unspoiled nature.

Friday Evening

Many visitors to Key West head directly to the festering entertainment district of Duval Street and start partying immediately. I suggest first checking in at one of the interesting **boutique hotels in Old Town** before setting out to debauch.

My favorite is the **Marquesa Hotel** on Fleming street. I also like the atmosphere at the quaint **Dewey House,** located at the quiet end of Duval Street. The more adventurous may select one of the many interesting **gay-oriented guesthouses** like **Alexander's Guest House**. See *Best Sleeps & Eats* for more details on these and other B&Bs, boutique hotels and resorts.

Assuming you arrive in time,

after checking in at your hotel, a drink at a salubrious bar before dinner is just the thing to get into the Key West mood.

The bars along Duval Street lure most visitors within minutes of their arrival in town. No problem. If you must do the gringo tourist thing and visit **Margaritaville** or the **Hard Rock**, try to get there early before the dinner crowds. Then have your drink, buy the T-shirt and shot glass and get out. *Don't eat there.* There are sooo many other places to eat in town that are waaay better.

Around sunset time, everyone heads to **Sunset Pier** for the evening ritual of ogling fellow tourists, **weird street performers** and the **sunset**— not necessarily in that order. You do have to do it at least one evening while you're in town.

SIGHTS

The hilarious duo **Pete & Wayne** usually do their obscenely funny act at **Sloppy Joe's** in the early evening starting at 5:30. Don't miss it. It's by far the best show in town. I suggest catching them on the first night—you'll probably want to catch them all the other nights you're in town also.

Dinner choices are huge, and seafood is the star of the show. If you haven't had your fill of Duval Street, **Mangoes** is a good spot for interesting sauces on fresh local seafood and a good view of the strange things happening on the street. For a memorable fine dining experience, try **Café Solé** on Southard Street at Frances, for grouper, yellowtail and hog snapper. Reserve in advance and request one of the garden tables. See *Best Sleeps & Eats* for information about these and other delightful places to eat in Key West.

Ready to party now? After dinner, you could head to one of seemingly thousands of clubs and bars. My favorite is the down-market **Green Parrot**. They feature the same drinks and beer available all over the island and good live

PARROTHEADS

What's all this I keep hearing about *parrotheads*? Because of his penchant for tropical themes in his music and writing, Jimmy Buffet fans (almost all fanatical) are known as parrotheads. Stop by Jimmy's Key West watering hole **Margaritaville** and you can be one too.

bands—often top touring blues acts. The **Afterdeck Bar** in Louie's Backyard is another good spot but likely to be crowded.

Things get "fun" in the tourist-oriented bars along Duval Street, but don't expect great drinks or great live music. You can find both but it's not the usual thing. Young and not so young crowds pack the **Hog's Breath** for wet T-shirt contests and other culturally interesting activities. If you are so inclined, the Garden of Eden is upstairs at the Bull & Whistle. Check out their **Naked Sunset happy hour** and other, even more appealing, late-night events.

Saturday

It's easy to **rent a bike** or **moped** to zip around town, but beware of drinking even

SIGHTS

mild alcoholic beverages while operating any sort of vehicle—even a bicycle. **Paradise Scooter Rentals** rents bikes and scooters. The scooters run around $25 an hour or $60 for all day. They have a booth at 430 Duval Street.

It's hard to beat the twee **Old Towne Trolley** for getting a quick orientation tour around town and find out quickly what's of interest for you. The silly trolleys leave from Mallory Square. The **Conch Train** is another, even cornier option. Put on your fanny pack and go for it.

A great way to spend half a day (or many days) is to get out on the water to enjoy the nearby, spectacular coral reefs for **snorkeling**, **scuba diving** or **fishing**. The sea around Key West has some of the finest and most pristine remaining coral reefs in North America. **Blue Water Charters** specializes in scuba, snorkeling and fishing trips to some of the more remote and obscure sites and can create custom trips for small groups.

If water sports are not your thing, make a quick shopping trip down Duval Street to buy resort wear and gifts for the grandkids back home. Try **Summersalt** on Front Street or **Tropical Wave** on Duval for tank tops, Ts, sandals, bathing suits and tropical resort wear. Yes, the tykes need Jimmy Buffett shirts too.

There are dozens of attractions and distractions in Key West. Most are pretty cheesy but some are fun anyway. I particularly like the **Key West Aquarium** on Whitehead Street. I head immediately to the shark cage in the back to check out the big boys and then start my tour of the small tanks full of reef fish.

Audubon House & Tropical Gardens shows visitors 28 first edition works. For serious birders, this is a holy shrine. It's a very nice, small museum with a pleasant gift shop and lovely tropical garden.

SIGHTS

Key West has a couple of good beaches. **County Beach** on Atlantic Avenue (more or less at the far end of Duval Street) is loaded with public beach amenities like volleyball and food stands. There's not any surf to speak of, but you can snorkel a little bit or just walk around soaking up the sun and sights.

Old Town Key West is a wonderful place to walk or ride around and marvel at the old homes from another, perhaps more gracious time. **Lloyd's Original Key West Bike Tours** is the easiest way to do this. Mr. Lloyd leads guided bike tours through the scenic back streets and popular tourist areas of Key West, specializing in keeping kids fascinated.

Lunch in Key West is a wonderful topic to tell you about. If you like seafood, I suggest using lunch as an excuse to try out juicy fish sandwiches and sample conch fritters. Maybe scarf down some crab or Key West pinks (local shrimp) - nothing fancy. See *Best Sleeps & Eats* for my favorites.

Summer afternoons in Key West are usually spent either in a bar or near a pool. Other times of the year it is cool enough all day to get out and about. Even so, the pool and bar thing usually wins out. There are still plenty of things to do and see if you have the energy.

The beautiful old **Harry S. Truman Little White House** is wonderfully maintained and loaded with historically significant items. The atmosphere is just like the old days. Guides schooled in the most trivial of Truman trivia lead informative tours. The tour I was on included a real Truman nerd who tried hard to stump the guide. Couldn't be done.

Ernest Hemingway Home & Museum on Whitehead Street has an extra, odd attraction: cats with too many toes. The Hemingway cats have been inbreeding for so long they have little oddities (like too many toes) that endear them to the tourist public. The house is full of memorabilia. The 75+ cats are mostly in the garden. They are open every day of the year.

During the day, as you walk around town shopping with the wife or whatever, select a couple of likely looking spots for the enjoyment of tropical adult beverages or beer for later. Duval Street has plenty. I suggest spending the last part of the afternoon sloshing around the **Schooner Wharf Bar** on William Street before the dinner crowd shows up and clogs things up. You might even get a seat where you can see the sunset. Wheeee!

As the day draws to a close you may find you have to choose between spending the sunset hour **drinking at Sloppy Joe's** chortling to **Pete & Wayne's** sparkling nasty humor or rubbing shoulders and fanny packs with others of your ilk **watching the sunset** at the sea wall by Sunset Pier. Both happen about the same time. Both places will be heaving on Saturday evening.

Nightlife choices in Key West range from quiet or rowdy, tiki hut or trendy, straight or gay. Just walking up and down Duval Street on a Saturday night is entertainment enough for almost anyone. You will surely encounter beautiful girls all dressed up fancy who accost you familiarly on the street—they may not really be girls. They're taking the Mickey. Enjoy – you're part of the show too. See *Best Nightlife* for my picks.

Crawl back to your quaint B&B or hotel and sleep the sleep of the just.

Sunday
It's a pretty long haul back to Miami, but don't worry about that until mid- or even late-afternoon — there's still plenty to do: take the rental bike

SIGHTS

back, do some last minute shopping, try the conch fritters at Mangoes one more time.

On the way back to Miami, stop for coffee at **Baby's** (MM 15 OS) and have dinner at **Whale Harbor Inn** (MM 83.9 OS) or **Alabama Jack's** for one last taste of the Keys. Keep someone sober for the drive back and drive *slowwww*. There are long stretches of two-lane highway. Nighttime driving here can be monotonous. Avoid head-on collisions.

A WEEK IN KEY WEST

An entire week in Key West! Fantasy Fest, Spring Break, Hemingway Days and dozens of other festivals lure visitors. The partying in Key West is topped only by the wonderful fishing, diving and kayaking in the subtropical wilderness around the island. A week is plenty of time, but still not enough.

Day One

If you are driving down, get out of Miami as quickly as you can. See *Practical Matters* for the best route out of town. Avoid US 1 until you get south of Homestead. If you take the catamaran ferry from Miami or fly into the Key West airport, just taxi to your quaint lodgings in Old Town and unload.

Drive slow along the Overseas Highway. The traffic is pretty thick at times and there are bountiful radar traps for separating the unwary tourist from their dollars.

As soon as you arrive in Key West, check into one of the fabulous Old Town historic homes that have been converted into **fashionable boutique hotels** and **hip gay guesthouses**. Choose the leafy part of Key West: **Old Town**. It's close to the action and oozes charm.

See *Best Sleeps & Eats* for my picks on where to stay and dine. Relax, walk around Duval Street, pick a nice place to eat, then if you're not too tired hit some of those bars for which Key West is so famous. For details, see my *Best Nightlife* section.

Days Two – Six
You have five full days for shopping, drinking, eating, fishing, scuba diving or snorkeling, kayaking, gawking at tourist attractions and dozens of other things to do around Key West. Don't miss a seaplane or boat trip to the **Dry Tortugas** to see the beautiful **Fort Jefferson** (*photo below*).

For not much more than you would spend for an afternoon eating lunch and drinking, you can visit nearby Fort Jefferson in the Dry Tortugas. The trip by boat features a bar and buffet, so you won't come up short.

Paradise Scooter Rentals rents bikes and scooters. It's easy to **rent a bike** or **moped** to zip around town but be-

CRUISE SHIP CROWDS

Dozens of cruise ships now stop in Key West, disgorging massive hordes of first-time travelers who mingle uneasily with the town's hipper traditional visitors. Duval Street bars, restaurants and T-shirt shops can be packed. Wednesdays, Saturdays and Sundays are usually the days with the least cruise-ship traffic.

ware of drinking even mild alcoholic beverages while operating any sort of vehicle—even a bicycle. The scooters run around $25 an hour or $60 for all day. They have a booth at 430 Duval Street.

Put on your fanny pack and go for it. It's hard to beat the twee **Conch Train** for getting a quick orientation tour around town and find out quickly what's of interest for you. The silly trains leave from Mallory Square. The **Old**

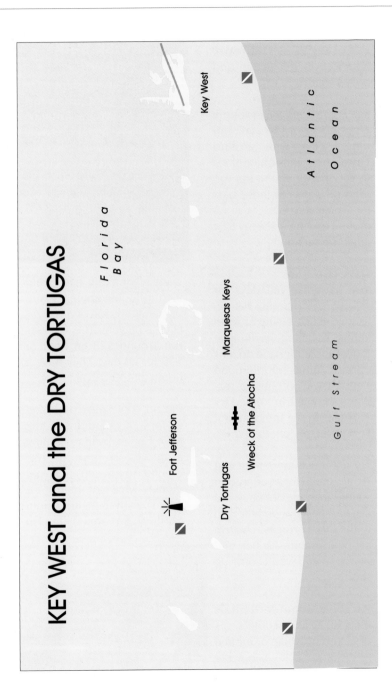

KEY WEST and the DRY TORTUGAS

Florida Bay

Key West

Marquesas Keys

Wreck of the Atocha

Fort Jefferson

Dry Tortugas

Atlantic Ocean

Gulf Stream

SIGHTS

Towne Trolley is another option.

The sea around Key West is the home of some of the finest and most pristine remaining coral reefs in North America. A great way to spend half a day (or many days) is to get out on the water to enjoy the nearby, spectacular coral reefs for **snorkeling, scuba diving or fishing. Blue Water Charters** specializes in scuba, snorkeling and fishing trips to some of the more remote and obscure sites, and can create custom trips for small groups.

On the **Discovery Glass Bottom Boat**, you can keep your feet dry and still experience spectacular coral gardens. The reefs off Key West are some of the most spectacular in the world, and it would be a shame to miss them just because you can't get in the water for one reason or another. The Discovery offers three trips a day.

County Beach on Atlantic Avenue (more or less at the far end of Duval Street) is loaded with public beach amenities like volleyball and food stands. There's not any surf to speak of, but you can snorkel a little bit or just walk around soaking up the sun and sights.

Lloyd's Original Key West Bike Tours is the most talked-about tour in Key West. Mr. Lloyd leads guided bike tours through the scenic back streets and popular tourist areas of Key West, specializing in keeping kids fascinated. He makes several stops to sample fresh fruit picked from trees along the route.

A kayaking trip is not to be missed if you like the outdoors. Nearby **Florida Bay** and **Everglades National Park,** have hundreds of square miles of turtle grass and sand flats dotted with small mangrove keys. **Lazy Dog Outfitters** rents all sorts of kayaks and fun watercraft. If you're into kayak fishing, this is the place.

Wild Dolphin Adventures takes you snorkeling just off-

SIGHTS

shore in places where those frisky wild dolphins come to play. These guys are not in cages. They're not going to let you scratch 'em on the tummy and ride along holding onto a fin, but they do get close enough for you to appreciate just how free and athletic they really are. *If you want to mess around with dolphins, this is the way to do it.* Those roadside dolphin attractions you saw driving down through the keys are bad mojo. They charge tourists to swim with imprisoned dolphins. They're going to go to Hell.

Even if you're not the active outdoorsy type, you still have a big selection of activities for a day of fun.

There are dozens of attractions and distractions in Key West. Most are pretty cheesy, but some are fun anyway. I particularly like the **Key West Aquarium** on Whitehead Street. I head immediately to the shark cage in the back to check out the big boys, and then start my tour of the small tanks full of reef fish.

Audubon House & Tropical Gardens on Whitehead Street

shows visitors 28 first edition works. For serious birders, this is a holy shrine. It's a very nice, small museum with a pleasant gift shop and lovely, tropical garden.

The beautiful old **Harry S. Truman Little White House** is wonderfully maintained and loaded with historically significant items. The atmosphere is just like it was in the old days. Guides schooled in the most trivial of Truman trivia lead informative tours. The tour I was on included a real Truman nerd who tried hard to stump the guide. Couldn't be done.

Ernest Hemingway Home & Museum on Whitehead Street has an extra, odd attraction: cats with too many toes. The Hemingway cats have been inbreeding for so long they have little oddities (like too many toes) that endear them to the tourist public. The house is full of memorabilia. The 75+ cats are mostly in the garden. The museum is open every day of the year.

Schooner Warf is conveniently located, as you could just crawl from the bar to the next event: a sunset cruise on

SIGHTS

the **Schooner Appledore Champagne Sunset Sail**. Yes, it's a little touristy, but you get to putt around the harbor a little and see the scene at Sunset Pier from a somewhat different perspective (and a safe distance).

Make a quick shopping trip down Duval Street to buy resort wear and gifts for the grandkids back home. Try **Summersalt** on Front Street or **Tropical Wave** on Duval Street for tank tops, Ts, sandals, bathing suits and all manner of tropical resort wear. Yes, the tykes need Jimmy Buffett shirts too. And watch out for the high-pressure bait and switch tactics at some of the loud T-shirt shops.

Last Day
Drive home, with some stops along the way to fuel your drive back to Miami.

Not far out of Key West you'll pass **Baby's** on the ocean side. Definitely stop here for the full-on coffee experience. Stop and have dinner at **Whale Harbor Inn** or **Alabama Jack's** for one last taste of the Keys.

BEST SLEEPS & EATS

Key West has a great selection of interesting places to stay. There are regular old motel-style places where you can rent a basic room and join in the general party that is always going on. There are upscale places, including the Hilton and the Crowne Plaza, which are much like the other quality hotels with those prestigious names. However, the best and most interesting lodging options are the dozens of old houses that have been converted to B&Bs, boutique hotels and guesthouses. The Old Town neighborhood is quaint and located right next to the action. The whole area drips with history. If you possibly can, you should stretch your budget to include a stay in one of Key West's famous converted Old Town homes.

Among other things, Key West is famous for gay- and lesbian-tolerant or gay- or lesbian-only guesthouse,s and charming B&Bs. The stories are all true. Almost any lodging in Key West will be gay-friendly, and a few are gay- or lesbian-only (one property advertises a policy of "no children, dogs or men"). Unless you want to associate only with people of your own sexual persuasion, or want to enjoy the clothing-optional areas (such as pools, lounges, and video rooms), I really don't think there is any need to make your lodging selection based on the gay policies of any particular property. However, these famous properties exude atmosphere and sexual mystique and draw interested, and sometimes interesting, visitors.

Alexander's Guest House $$$

Alexander's is considered to be the nicest of the gay guesthouses Key West is so famous for. It has a reputation for being oriented not so much towards cruising as simply being a comfortable place for couples to stay and perhaps mingle. Places to mingle include the clothing-optional pool, spa, yoga classes, breakfast buffet, afternoon wine & cheese or one of the three sundecks. They have free wireless. It's about five or six blocks from Duval Street. *Info: 1118 Flemming Street. www.alexghouse.com; Tel. 305-294-9919.*

BEST OF THE BEST IN KEY WEST

Sunset Key Guest Cottages $$$$

Just a few hundred yards off Key West, and reachable only by launch, is the super-exclusive Sunset Key Guest Cottages. On 27 acres of luxury, the resort island offers guests solid four-star treatment at five star prices. Rooms and amenities are, for the most part, top of the line luxury. The one-, two-, and three-bedroom cottages are scattered around the island, with a wonderful pool snaking through the middle. The lush tropical plantings are rivaled only by the delicious tropical beverages cranked out by the bar staff. Room service and private chef services are available. You can get back and forth from Key West by launch 24 hours a day. Very convenient to the festering lunacy of Key West yet confidently isolated from that wonderful madness. Westin is the current owner. *Info: 245 Front Street. www.westinsunsetkeycottages.com; Tel. 305-292-5300.*

Atlantic Shores Resort $$

Definitely not upscale, the Shores is a great place to stay if you're looking for a very lively, party atmosphere. This "resort" features such amenities as a clothing-optional pool with bar, and an onsite liquor store. *Info: 510 South Street. www.atlanticshoresresort.com; Tel. 305-296-2491, 888-324-2995.*

Azul Key West $$$

This meticulously renovated 19th century Queen Anne-style conch house, originally built by a wealthy cigar baron for his son and new bride, has been lovingly crafted into an 11-room boutique hotel. It's located a few blocks from the south end of Duvall. Rooms are equipped with the nice linens, luxurious

SLEEPS & EATS

toiletries, flat screen and in-room wi-fi. They have a nice pool and supply a nice spread of breads, pastries, cereal and interesting fruits for breakfast. Very civilized. Adults only. *Info: 907 Truman Avenue. www.azulkeywest.com; Tel. 305-296-5152, 800-253-2985.*

Banyan Resort $$$$

The buildings of the Banyan Resort are a collection of nicely renovated old Key West homes with a designation from the National Register of Historic Places. The location is superb. It's only a block from Duval Street and just a little farther from Mallory Square. There's a pleasant pool with a tiki bar serving wonderful rum punch. You might even get an umbrella in your drink. The chickens in the neighborhood serve as an alarm clock, but that's just part of the Old Key West charm. The pool can be noisy, but in general the place is quiet in spite of being so close to the party parts of town. Some of the units have kitchenettes. It's quite nice—comfortable and upscale—but not in the luxury category. *Info: 323 Whitehead Street. www.thebanyanresort.com; Tel. 305-296-7786.*

Big Ruby's Guesthouse $$$

A member of the World's Foremost Gay and Lesbian Hotels, Big Ruby's is one of the more famous of the tolerant Key West guesthouses. A bit more upscale than most of the others, Big Ruby's is also conveniently located, less than a block from Duval Street. The lagoon-style pool is one of the nicest ones in town, surrounded with tropical plantings and little corners to hang out in. They have a large Jacuzzi and fitness center. Breakfast and complimentary wine in the evenings are part of the deal. *Info: 409 Applerouth Lane. www.bigrubys.com; Tel. 305-296-2323.*

GETTING NAKED

Everybody always wants to know if it's okay to go around naked in the Keys. No. It's not. There are a few nude beaches (mentioned in the "Beaches" sections), and things can get a little weird in Key West on Duval Street during some of the rowdier festivals. At times, wearing not much more than spray paint is not "nude." Just don't push it.

Blue Parrot Inn B&B $$$

The pet-friendly Blue Parrot is conveniently located near Seven Fish, one of my favorite Key West eateries. It's also only a couple of blocks from Duval Street. The Blue Parrot consists of a group of quaint, carefully restored Old Town Key West homes built in 1884. There is a pool and extraordinary tropical plantings. They do a solid poolside breakfast. If you are a cat lover you will be assigned your very own cat for the duration of your stay. This cat to sleep at the foot of your bed, purrs, sleeps a lot and probably whines for something to eat. Nice. *Info: 916 Elizabeth Street. www.blueparrotinn.com; Tel. 305-296-0033.*

Center Court Historic Inn & Cottages $$$$

The upscale Center Court is a collection of historic and charming Old Town Key West houses, cottages, suites and rooms. Some of the cottages have their own private pools for honeymooners or others with romantic ideas. Pets and kids are welcome. In fact, a couple of friendly dogs lurk about. The Jack Russell runs frantically around the pool having fun while the lab sleeps. Sounds about right. They require a minimum stay of five nights. It's a little stuffy but nicely done. *Info: 915 Center Street. www.centercourtkw.com; Tel. 305-296-9292.*

Chelsea House Pool & Gardens $$$

The amenities at this adults-only guesthouse include a pool, a clothing-optional rooftop deck, and wireless internet service (which works well only in the lobby). It's only a few blocks from Duval Street, and there's good parking (important). The neighborhood roosters have no idea what time it is. The front rooms are the noisiest. Pet-friendly.  Overall, this place is nice, but the breakfast is famously poor. *Info: 709 Truman Avenue. www.historickeywestinns.com; Tel. 800-845-8859.*

SLEEPS & EATS

Dewey House $$$$

Operated by Old Town Resorts, this historic old house is smartly

run, upscale and nicely located, if a little on the sterile side. They have a lovely breakfast in the morning and snacks in the afternoon. Very civilized, but somehow lacking in funky charm. *Info: 506 South Street. www.oldtownresorts.com; Tel. 305-296-6577.*

Marquesa Hotel $$$$

This well run boutique hotel consists of a group of restored Old Key West homes set around pools and wonderful tropical plantings. Each room is different, having been shoehorned into the old buildings without sacrificing much of the architectural

value. Some rooms and suites are definitely nicer than others, but all are very well appointed and even quirky. Their restaurant of the same name is one of the nicest fine dining opportunities in the Keys. *Info: 600 Fleming Street. www.marquesa.com; Tel. 305-292-1919.*

Santa Maria Suites $$$$

At the end of Simonton Street, the newly upgraded and Santa Maria Suites are under new management and doing well. The location is quiet with rooms grouped around a large pool. The suites are stunning and come equipped with every high-end amenity and gadget you could desire. The kitchens are high-style with wine refrigerators and Cuisinart blenders, specialized lobster and crab cooking and eating tools, and more. The two bedrooms each with full bath make this a great choice for a family or for two couples wanting elegance and cooking facilities.

Service is over the top with fresh pastries and ice cream delivered every night as part of the turn down service. This is not Olde Key West—more Miami Beach but elegant and comfortable. It is one of my top picks in Key West. *Info: 1401 Simonton Street. www.santamariasuites.com; Tel. 305-600-5165.*

Southernmost Hotel $$$

Although this motel-style property has been around since the early days of Key West tourism, it's modern and stylish, and the rooms are well appointed and luxurious. The location at the end of Duval Street is great—close to the action yet quiet. The grounds are well maintained, and the rooms have all been recently and thoroughly renovated. They come with all the goodies. My only complaint is that the place is so popular that the pool and grounds seem a bit crowded at times. One big benefit of staying here is the guarded parking lot right in front. Convenient and comfortable. Once again, Old Town Resorts runs a tight ship. *Info: 1319 Duval Street. www.oldtownresorts.com; Tel. 305-296-6577.*

A & B Lobster House $$

This is an old favorite for crab, lobster (Maine and Florida), steaks and specials. They try to get fancy with fine cognac and cigars, but the food is simply okay. Most of it seems to have been quickly heated up just after being delivered by the Sysco truck. Same old steamed vegetables. *Info: 700 Front Street. www.aandblobsterhouse.com; Tel. 305-294-5880.*

SLEEPS & EATS

DINING OUT IN KEY WEST

You don't have to spend a lot of money to eat well in Key West. But it helps. Restaurants in Key West practice gastronomy involving a wonderful assortment of fresh seafood, and build a menu based on a fusion/mix/mash/mess or miracle of every conceivable US/Mexican/Asian/European/tropical/down-home style that sells to the swarms of hungry tourists. This is a good thing. On the other hand, a few restaurants sell simple fresh seafood with little makeup or frou-frou.

One of the most important things about eating in Key West is the joy of dining, drinking or simply lounging about in a bar or restaurant overlooking watching the milling crowds on Duval Street. Shameless people watching while eating spicy bar food and guzzling brightly colored holiday drinks—great fun. I particularly like to get an upstairs table at one of the restaurants with a balcony overlooking Duval. At that height, the people on the street don't realize you're there, so you can brazenly stare as the weird Duval Street parade passes just underneath your feet.

Antonia's $$$

Nice ambiance with all the usual Italian pasta specials. The steak with balsamic drizzle and goat cheese is terrific. Try the cookies and port after the meal. The Duval location is another plus. *Info: 615 Duval Street. www.antoniaskeywest.com; Tel. 305-294-6565.*

B.O.'s Fish Wagon $

Huge grouper sandwiches are a very big part of the Key West experience, and everyone (but me) says B.O.'s makes the best ones on the island. I find the sandwiches to be dry with a medium-sized, deep fried piece of fish served on a plain white bun. If you put a bunch of lime and tartar sauce on it you will be okay. I really cannot understand why anyone would think these guys are anything special. Try the conch fritters. *Info: 801 Caroline Street. Tel. 305-294-9272.*

Café Marquesa $$$$

Very highly rated, this is one of the best of the Keys' fine dining establishments. It's just a little place with a small bar popular with local characters but the food and wine list are famous. Arugula salad with goat cheese, duck, lamb chops and ginger almond coconut encrusted grouper

are typical menu items. *Info: 600 Fleming Street at the Marquesa Hotel. Tel. 305-292-1244.*

Café Solé $$$$

Very popular with the food press and upscale diners, this is one of the best places to enjoy local seafood fused with the latest, trendiest Key West flavors. This should definitely be on your list of dinner spots for your time in Key West. Some of the tables are outside in the garden. Very romantic. Reserve well in advance (a month or more) if you want to dine surrounded by tropical flowers. Bouillabaise, hog snapper (a very tasty fish seldom seen in restaurants but probably the tastiest of all the snapper family), and grouper are typical entrees. I have heard a few reports of substandard service lately. *Info: 1029 Southard Street at Frances. www.cafesole.com; Tel. 305-294-0230.*

Conch Town (formerly Johnson's) Café $

This is one of my all-time favorite Key West places to eat. It's just a little window on a guy's front porch with a menu on a board out front. An old black guy cooks everything up for each order. The fish sandwiches are the kind that drip juice off your arm and are huge. Watch the hot sauce. The conch fritters come hot from the oil, served in paper. They don't get any better. If you don't like the conch fritters here, you should just give up on them completely and go back to chicken nuggets. Go next door for the fish and grits on Sunday mornings. *Info: 801 Thomas Street. Tel. 305-292-2286.*

SLEEPS & EATS

El Mesón De Pepe $$

Mojitos and live Latin sounds keep the place lively. It's usually busy with young trendies scarfing sort-of-Cuban food. *Info: 410 Wall Street. Tel. 305-295-2620.*

El Siboney $

Cuban-American food at regular prices. Good stuff. Stews, pork, beef, fried plantains, rice & beans. They don't do mojitos or margaritas in plastic cups. This is just good eating like at your grandmother's house in Miami. No credit cards. *Info: 900 Catherine Street. www.elsiboneyrestaurant.com; Tel. 305-296-4184.*

Hogfish Bar & Grill $

With no pretensions, no hype and mostly locals, the Hogfish prides itself on its great food and lack of, well, pride. Hogfish sandwiches are legendary. Also try their lobster BLT and fish tacos. They almost always have Key West pinks ready, hot or cold. *Info: 6810 Front Street, Stock Island. www.hogfishbar.com. Tel. 305-293-4041.*

Mangoes Restaurant And Catering $$$

The best thing about Mangoes is the location right on Duval Street. It's hard to beat for people-watching. If you can get a table near the front, you can enjoy quite good seafood specials and the passing parade of strange Key West denizens and tourists. Pecan-encrusted yellowtail, grouper with coconut sauce, guava-barbequed prawns and the like are typical menu items. Get this: they have their own pastry chef! *Info: 700 Duval Street. Tel. 305-292-4606.*

SQUARE GROUPER

You'll probably hear the expression "square grouper" used in the Keys from time to time. It refers to a largish bale of smuggler-jettisoned pot (or cocaine) floating around in the sea—the preferred catch of many local commercial fishermen. Now you know.

Nasty Burger $

From time to time, the old guy living at 308 Petronia tacks a small menu on his door and begins selling his special: nasty burgers. That's all he sells. No chicken nuggets or any of that crap. Just nasty burgers. He can go for months without opening up. The only way to get a nasty burger is to stroll by from time to time until you happen to find the place open. Normally I would not include a place like this since it is so unreliable, but the burgers are extremely reliable: good! *Info: 308 Petronia Street. No phone.*

Santiago's $$

Not far past the unremarkable Blue Heaven is a small tapas restaurant with wonderful ceviche, sangria, chorizo, albóndigas (meatballs in sauce), pinchos morunos, and the classic, gambas en ajillo (shrimp in garlic). They have some nice Spanish wines including a couple of refreshing cavas. *Info: 207 Petronia Street. www.santiagosbodega.com; Tel. 305-296-7691.*

KEY LIME PIE
Every restaurant in Florida serves "Key lime pie," but few diners are aware that Key limes are smaller, yellower and milder than the familiar green limes you find in the grocery store. The best pies are yellow (rare)—the natural color of Key lime juice. Green pies have been dyed. Reject them. They have probably been made from ordinary limes (or bought frozen from Sysco). Most key limes are gown in Brazil rather than actually in the keys.

Seven Fish $$$$

The times I have eaten here, they had less than five types of fish on offer, but I can't really complain, because everything I have been served here has been wonderful. Gnocchi with creamy blue cheese sauce (it varies night to night) is one of my favorites. They only serve fresh local fish and shrimp. That means grouper, mahi, cobia, wahoo, tuna, bar jack, and mackerel. The style is the usual fusion of tropical ingredients and Asian flavors. They also have wonderful steaks, mixed grills and, of all things, to die for meatloaf. The atmosphere is more small-town café than gourmet dining, but the quality of the food tops all. They have a long list of wines by the glass - mostly whites, no surprise. My only possible complaint is the lack of any Spanish wines, currently booming in popularity among wine cognoscenti. But still, Seven Fish is absolutely wonderful! This is without a doubt my favorite restaurant in Key West. *Info: 632 Olivia Street. www.7fish.com; Tel. 305-296-2777.*

BEST SHOPPING

The tourist shopping available in Key West is rivaled only by the scene in the Cayman Islands or Nassau. Basically, any tourist item you might desire is here (especially if it is fish- or Buffett-themed). Watch out for the old bait-and-switch trick perpetrated by some of the shops along Duval Street. They use the loud music and confusion at the cash register to sell you $20 T-shirts instead of the $2 shirts you thought you were buying.

Hard Rock, Margaritaville and other big tourist traps sell all the expected crap: shot glasses, signature T-shirts, pins, hats, Elvis paperweights and other junk. Go for it. You are a tourist aren't you? You know you want to.

Key West Island Books
This is a good bookstore. They had all of my books the last time I was there. As they are not a chain, they seem to use a little more imagination when selecting titles to stock. They have the best selection of local authors and books about Key West and the Keys you are likely to find anywhere. Buy your books here. It's locally owned. *Info: 513 Fleming Street. www.keywest islandbookts.com; Tel. 305-294-2904.*

Walden's Books
They have a decent selection of local titles, but you simply won't find some of the more interesting titles you can see in the locally owned Key West Island Books on Fleming. *Info: 2212 North Roosevelt Boulevard. Tel. 305-294-5419.*

Valladares and Son

Hemingway, Tennessee Williams and Harry Truman (but *not* Jimmy Buffett) bought their morning paper here, so you should too. They have a good selection of books with local color. *Info: 1200 Duval Street. Tel. 305-296-5032.*

Kermit's Key West Lime Shoppe

Many people say that this is the place to get the best Key Lime pie in the Keys. Lots of people say this about lots of pie shoppes, but these guys do make a good pie. They sell Key lime jams, sauces, syrup and all manner of limey gifts. *Info: Corner of Green and Elizabeth Streets. www.keylimeshop.com; Tel. 305-296-0806.*

Key West Pearl Co.

Although no pearls actually come from the waters around Key West (except for inferior ones from conchs), it seems to be a good place to sell them to the tourist hordes. Natural American pearls, Tahitian black pearls, and natural conch pearls are on offer. They also have a selection of 14k gold pearl jewelry. *Info: Front Street. www.keywestpearl.com; Tel. 305-295-6780.*

KEY WEST CIGARS

Key West has a long history of rolling cigars. Tampa eventually lured most of the cigar makers away with subsidies and tax increment financing, but you can still buy hand-rolled cigars at booths on Duval Street. If you must smoke a stogie and you don't do it all the time, buy small ones so you don't have to feel bad about throwing away a perfectly good, half-smoked cigar before you hurl. Do not inhale. Don't swallow your saliva either.

Kino Sandals

This is sandal heaven for the sandal set. They make them right in the shop. All natural materials are used and almost all of the work is done by hand. Groovy. *Info: Fitzpatrick Street. www.kinosandals.com; Tel. 305-294-5044.*

Peppers of Key West

This is the place to buy your

SHOPPING

hot sauce. Hot sauces from around the world are on the shelves along with hot jellies, jams and other hot things. Join their hot sauce of the month club. Approach with caution. *Info: Greene Street. Tel. 800-KW SAUCE.*

Scrubs of Key West
Oddly, tropical fashions for medical professionals are the new thing for hip hospital personnel. They have a rather amazing collection. I'm not sure if I would feel good about my anesthesiologist if they were wearing a Jimmy Buffett shirt, but there's no accounting for

tastes. *Info: Caroline Street. www.scrubskeywest.com; Tel. 305-853-1700*

Summersalt
Tank tops, Ts, sandals, bathing suits and all manner of tropical resort wear are on sale here. Visit when you first get to Key West so you'll be ready to party in style. *Info: Front Street. Tel. 305-294-4974.*

Tropical Wave
Tropical resort wear for women and children. Yes, the tykes need Jimmy Buffett shirts too. *Info: Duval Street. Tel. 305-296-5550.*

BEST NIGHTLIFE & ENTERTAINMENT

Get naked and walk down the street drinking beer. Sound crazy? Few people would want *me* to do anything like that but, if you paint yourself up right and smile, you can do just that during some of the livelier festivals in Key West. If you like to party more sedately, that can also be arranged. Key West is a famous party town with notorious establishments like **Sloppy Joe's**, the **Hog's Breath**, **Margaritaville** and the wonderful blues haven the **Green**

Parrot. Gay travelers come for the permissive atmosphere and gay-friendly guesthouses and clubs.

Key West has approximately 200 bars, and they are all ready for you. Loud bars, quiet bars, gay bars, sad bars. Personally I like the **Green Parrot** and **Sloppy Joe's**, but any place that's on the water or that has good music will do.

Key West is famous around the world for her nightlife,

and by no means all the action happens by night. At many places, the live music starts early in the afternoon. You won't hear the sort of sophisticated musicals or jazz bands that are highlights in other music towns such as New York. Key West's musical pleasures are more casual. The typical Keys entertainer sports an acoustic guitar, long gray hair and no shoes. The typical repertoire is a beachy mix of well-known rock, folk, country and blues favorites. Audience sing-alongs, boozy patter and incitements to drunkenness and partial nudity are all part of the show. You can catch this kind of local fun at any of the bars around Duval, any evening of the week. A handful of places, including the Green Parrot, Schooner Wharf, Sloppy Joe's, Margaritaville and the Hog's Breath, also feature touring regional rock and blues bands, some of which are excellent.

The most entertaining show in town is the hilarious duo **Pete & Wayne**, who hold forth at **Sloppy Joe's** Thursday through Sunday. Their raunchy parodies of popular songs feature adult language and

childish humor. These tequila-swilling equal-opportunity offenders aren't for everyone, but nobody typifies the Key West experience better. Another local legend that you do not want to miss is Barry Cuda, aka The Pianimal. This barrelhouse pianist puts on one heck of a show, solo or with a band. You may see him wheeling his piano down the street between gigs at Sloppy Joe's, the Hog's Breath and various other local bars.

Afterdeck Bar

This is the bar in Louie's Backyard. The cultured local elite and knowledgeable tourists choke the place most nights. If you can't afford to eat at Louie's, have a few drinks at the bar instead and skip dinner. Legend has it that Jimmy Buffet once played here for beer and tips. *Info: 700 Waddell Street in Louie's Backyard. www.louiesbackyard.com; Tel. 305-294-1061.*

NIGHTLIFE & ENTERTAINMENT

NIGHTLIFE & ENTERTAINMENT

WET T-SHIRT CONTESTS

A revered spring break ritual, wet T-shirt contests are a real hoot. But you have to be in the right frame of mind. Young, drunk or becoming drunk males and their soused dates are the target audience. Once the crowd is in the right mood, the action starts by auctioning off the right to be the guy who squirts the girls in the chest (or wherever) with a high-pressure water hose. I've seen this privilege go for over $100. Next, the contestants come up one by one to be soaked down, prance around strutting their stuff and get hollered at by the rowdy crowd who are by now hanging off trees and roofs of nearby buildings continuously hooting like apes. Some contestants are pros and some charming amateurs. The crowd can get waaay out of hand, aggressively exhorting "tits out!" This laddish behavior can result in some of the more naive contestants blushing (or even crying). Great fun!

Bull And Whistle Entertainment Complex

With four bars and live entertainment every day, the Bull seems to have it all. They have pool tables and, of course, an upstairs clothing-optional bar. Yes, you can drink beer in the buff. Clothing-optional means you can sit around drinking beer and eating bar snacks in the nude. I like to do this at home sometimes, but it's not really my thing to do so in a public bar. However, many who visit this freethinking island *are* interested in doing just that. The **Garden of Eden** is the place to do it. Located on the top floor, the Garden of Eden opens at 10am for the sun worshipers, and goes on until waaay late. Their "Naked Sunset" happy hour is world famous (sort of). This is the place to get your body painting done. They do a particularly "thorough" job, if you know what I mean. The best time to go is after 10pm. Jimmy Buffet never drank here. Neither did Hemingway. *Info: Corner of Caroline and Duval. Tel. 305-296-4565.*

Captain Tony's

This is the location of the original Sloppy Joe's where Hemingway hung. After some sort of argument about the rent, the bar owner, Tony, packed up everything in the middle of the night and hauled it down to the present Sloppy Joe's location. Other than that, Captain Tony's is just another bar. Jimmy Buffet drank here. *Info: 428 Green Street. Tel. 305-294-1838.*

Green Parrot

The best venue in Key West for good live music—especially blues. National and regional touring bands cycle through. It's got a nice, funky, redneck vibe and is not at all fancy. There are always lots of locals hanging about soaking up suds. *Info: 601 Whitehead Street. www.greenparrot.com; Tel. 305-294-6133.*

Hog's Breath Saloon

One of the rowdier bars along Duval. They have several live, occasionally good, performers every day. They hose mixed drinks into plastic cups at an astonishing rate. They make their own lager which is your best bet. The place to come for cultural events like wet T-shirt and homemade bikini contests. It's a hoot. *Info: 400 Front Street. www.hogsbreath.com; Tel. 305-296-4222.*

Pier House

Right at the end of Duval Street, the **Havana Docks Sunset Deck** is supposedly the hippest, best, coolest, and probably most expensive

place in Key West to watch the sunset hoping for the magic green glow. Ask the bartender about the green glow at sunset. That way he'll know you're hip. *Info: One Duval Street. Tel. 305-296-4600.*

PT'S Late Night Bar and Grill

Even though the kitchen now closes at 11pm or something like that, this is still about the best place to hang out in the wee hours. Unfortunately, they always have a half dozen or so TVs blaring out whatever sport is in season. *Info: 902 Caroline Street. Tel. 305-296-4245.*

Rick's

Dance, dance, dance to hip-hop, electronica and other contemporary sounds. Very hip scene last time I was in town. The coolest scene may be somewhere else by now. *Info: 200-300 Block of Duval Street. Tel. 305-296-4890.*

NIGHTLIFE & ENTERTAINMENT

Schooner Wharf Bar

A good bar with pleasant views, good seafood and honest drinks. The last time I was there they actually made the margaritas and daiquiris individually instead of dispensing them premixed from plastic hoses. They have live entertainment every night, some of it good. Key West icon Mike McCloud has been strumming the guitar here every afternoon for decades. The place is usually packed with tourists, and locals with their dogs. You'll love it. *Info: 202 William Street. www.schoonerwharf.com; Tel. 305-292-3302.*

Sloppy Joe's

Sloppy Joe's is by far the best of the Duval Street tourist joints. They usually have excellent live music. The hilarious childish adult humor duo **Pete & Wayne** entertain most of the year Thursday through Saturday evenings. *Don't miss*

these guys! You can check out the place on their web cam at www.peteandwayne.com. *Info: 201 Duval Street. www.sloppyjoes.com; Tel. 305-294-5717.*

Turtle Kraals Waterfront Bar

Featuring turtle races and other semi-interesting entertainment options, this is an unashamedly tourist-oriented drinking and music venue. Once a turtle slaughterhouse. It's been cleaned up slightly since then. They hose the place out every morning due to the high volume of beer and drinks they pump out from hoses every night to the thirsty tourist hordes. *Info: 231 Margaret Street at Land's End Marina. www.turtlekraals.com Tel. 305-294-2640.*

Wax

The best time to arrive at this snazzy, funky, techno, soul, big city lounge is probably sometime after 2am. That should tell you something. Chocotinis are not out of the question. This place used to be quite hip. There are definitely not many frat boys hanging out here. *Info: 422 Applerouth Lane. Tel. 305-304-6988.*

BEST SPORTS & RECREATION

Many visitors find elbow bending to be sport enough during their time in Key West, but they are missing some of the very best reasons to come to town.

DIVING & SNORKELING

Snorkeling and scuba diving conditions around Key West are the best in the US. There are miles of reefs with drop-offs, caves, sandy channels and all manner of exotic reef fish. The **Gulf Stream** is immediately adjacent to the reefs, bringing pelagic creatures close in for your viewing (and fishing) pleasure.

If you visit Key West and never get to snorkel, dive or fish in the waters around the island, you have missed one of the very best things about the island. Snorkeling and scuba diving are easy to do and there are many shops in the area ready to teach visitors so they can enjoy the spectacular reefs. The reefs are close by— you can easily do a morning or afternoon snorkel or scuba dive with loads of time and energy left over for elbow bending.

Western Dry Rocks is a great dive site that gets much less traffic than sites closer to Key West. It's worth a bit longer boat ride to get there. Look for lots of relatively pristine elkhorn and staghorn coral. Some big stuff swims by if you're looking in the right direction. Keep your eyes open at this site for pelagics, turtles and large rays.

For me, the best diving is done on the **outside reefs** that drop off from relatively shallow water to the depths of the Gulf Stream in just a few hundred feet. Currents can be an issue, but a good dive master will know the best times to go safely. There's a wide variety of reefs to choose from just a couple of miles offshore from Key West.

The wreck of the tugboat **Aquanaut** is one of the more popular wrecks close to Key West. Expect some big fish, including the inevitable Goliath grouper. It's in 75 feet of water in the middle of the sand with the edge of the Gulf Stream dropping off ominously in the distance. Spooky.

SPORTS & RECREATION

DIVING & FLYING

You don't want to get the bends at 30,000 feet on the flight back to Newark. This means it is a bad idea to scuba dive and fly on the same day. The pressurized cabins of modern airliners are usually pressurized at significantly less than sea level. If your body is still slowly expelling nitrogen absorbed while breathing compressed air on a recent dive, flying with a low atmospheric pressure could trigger problems that would not occur at sea level pressures. All this doesn't apply to snorkelers, because they don't breathe compressed air. **Scuba divers shouldn't dive within 24 hours before any flight.**

The nearby **Marquesas** and more distant **Dry Tortugas** are targets for divers willing to stay on live-aboard boats for several nights in order to get to remote, rarely-visited reefs and wrecks.

There are dozens of scuba and snorkeling operators. Here are my favorites in Key West:

The Subtropic Dive Center
These guys have two boats, and they run a morning and an afternoon trip on each. One boat is capable of carrying 42 sheep and the other 24. They do all the usual wreck and reef dives, as well as night dives. It costs about $95 for a two-tanker with all the gear. *Info: Garrison Bight. www.subtropic.com; Tel. 305-296-9914.*

Reef Raiders of Key West
Their smaller boat, the Reef Raider, is licensed for 24 passengers but only books 10 divers max. The larger boat, the Sea Breeze, is definitely in the cattle class, carrying 42 divers. Whew! They specialize in diving for the physically challenged. *Info: www.keywestscubadive.com; Tel. 866-563-1805.*

Dive Key West, Inc.
$120 gets you a half-day trip with all the gear. 16 divers go on the boat. They also have night dives. *Info: www.divekeywest.com; Tel 305-296-3823.*

Lost Reef Adventures
$90 gets you the full Monty for a half-day trip with 16 divers. Snorkeling costs a mere $40 all in. *Info:*

www.lostreefadventures.com; Tel 305-296-3823.

Blue Water Charters
Even though they are significantly more expensive than the other operators in town, these guys are the ones to go with if you are a serious diver. They take six people max. No cattle boats. They specialize in trips to some of the more remote and obscure sites, and can create custom trips for small groups. They offer trips focusing on spear fishing, photography, wreck diving and even fishing. *Info: www.bluewatercharterskey west.com; Tel. 305-304-8888.*

FISHING
There are several ways to enjoy fishing around Key West. The easiest, and the most likely to end up with you catching fish, is to charter a boat for the day. **Flats fishing** for bonefish, tarpon and permit is usually done in a small skiff with two guests - the guide poles the boat around the sand and turtle grass flats. **Trolling offshore** for billfish will more likely find you coming home with dorado (mahi) and wahoo for dinner but that's all right.

SNORKELING SAFETY
What's the biggest danger to snorkelers? Sting rays, eels, sharks, fire coral? Nope. None of those things will hurt you if you don't touch them, but the sun can hurt you badly if you aren't careful. Always wear a T-shirt when snorkeling. You'll be spending most of your time face-down floating on top of the water, with your back exposed to the broiling sun. You may also want to consider some waterproof sun block for your neck and legs. And remember, the Florida sun can burn you even on cloudy days.

Fishing around Key West is fantastic. Put down your beer glass, get up off your bar stool and get out on the water. Anglers up north spend their Saturday mornings in the winter hunched over their TVs watching their favorite fishing stars haul in **snook**, **trout**,

SPORTS & RECREATION

bonefish, **dorado** and other interesting game fish off Key West.

Key West is one of North America's top fishing destinations, with three main types of angling action. **Bones, permit, tarpon** and other exotics school up around the flats and channels. **Huge snapper, grouper, yellowtail** and **kingfish** swarm around the reefs. **Marlin, amberjack** and **sails** lurk just offshore in the Gulf Stream. The best tarpon months are April, May, and June. The bonefish are in the area year-round, but the best months are in the spring and fall.

There are dozens of fishing charters and guides. Here are my favorites in Key West:

Lazy Dog Outfitters
Formerly Hurricane Hole, these guys rent all sorts of kayaks and fun watercraft. If you're into kayak fishing, this is the place. They will pick you up at your hotel and take you out kayak fishing with all the proper gear. Half-day trips go for $85. They'll also cook your catch for your lunch or dinner back at the dock while plying you with cold beer. I like it. *Info: 5114 Overseas Hwy. www.lazydog.com; Tel. 305-295-9898.*

Captain Steven Lamp

This flats guide puts anglers on the bones, permit and tarpon. He has a couple of the nicer boats in the area and has been guiding locally for yonks. He specializes in fly-fishing techniques. *Info: Tel. 888-362-3474.*

Wild Bill
Specializing in trolling offshore for shark and sailfish, Wild Bill believes live bait is the best way to go. It's true. This is an indication that these guys are serious about actually catching fish, not just taking punters out for an expensive boat ride. *Info: Tel. 305-296-2533.*

Key Limey Charters
Deep sea trolling in the Gulf Stream for sails, dorado (mahi) and possibly a swordfish or tuna. Captain Murphy (a true limey) will get you there. *Info: www.lkeylimey.com; Tel. 305-293-1814.*

Dream Catcher Charters
Light tackle in the backcountry nets you tarpon, permit, shark, barracuda and cobia. Unlike most light tackle operations, Dream Catcher can take up to

four people on some of their boats. These guys specialize in very custom, including all nude, charters. Call for particulars. *Info: www.dreamcatchercharters.com; Tel. 305-292-7702.*

Tortuga IV

This party boat is a big, stable catamaran with an air-conditioned lounge. As usual, they supply bait and tackle, and will clean your catch, ready for the pan. You can come with nothing more than a good attitude and they'll fix you up. I suggest bringing sunscreen and a hat at least. Every Saturday night they have a special night fishing trip. *Info: www.tortugacharters.com; Tel. 305-293-1189.*

Gulf Stream III

Another party boat, the Gulf Stream docks at Garrison Bight. $50 gets you bait, tackle and a mate to bait your hook and take the fish off when you catch them. They clean them for you too. They do night fishing on Wednesdays. Info: Tel. 305-296-8494.

Andy Griffiths Charters

The best way to fish the more remote areas of the Keys, the Marquesas and the Dry Tortugas, is on one of the overnight boats. Andy Griffiths takes only six anglers for a two-night, three-day trip. You can fish all night if you like. *Info: www.fishandy.com; Tel. 305-296-2639.*

Fish Finder

Fish Finder is another economical way to get waaay out there for the best fishing. These guys take up to 36 anglers to the Dry Tortugas for two- or three-night trips. *Info: www.floridafishfinder.com; Tel. 800-878-FISH.*

BOATING

Renting a car while on vacation in an unfamiliar area is a great way to see the sights around you. Renting a boat in the Keys is much the same (as long as you know what you're doing). The best things about the Keys are in the water and you need a boat to get to them.

There is a wide variety of boat rental operators. Check their web sites and call in advance

SPORTS & RECREATION

to be sure they have the type of boat and equipment you need. Be sure to reserve well in advance. Some rental operators will deliver the boat if you are renting for several days.

Land's End Boat Rentals

Land's End rents all sorts of fun watercraft: jet skis, small fishing boats, runabouts and day sailors. There is a two-hour minimum rental. *Info: Key West. Tel. 305-294-6447.*

Schooner Liberty Clipper Day and Evening Sails

The Liberty is a modern replica of an 1800s freighter with all the big sails and rigging. They go out every afternoon for two hours at 2:30, leaving from behind the Westin Resort. *Info: Tel. 800-213-2474.*

Schooner Appledore Champagne Sunset Sail

The Appledore cruises past Sunset Pier exactly at sunset, so you can participate in the sunset festivities by having your picture taken by hundreds of tourists as you picturesquely sail by. Beer, wine, and champagne flow freely. If you like, you can haul on a rope or steer a little. Wheee! *Info: Tel. 800-213-2474.*

Discovery Glass Bottom Boat

The reefs off Key West are some of the most spectacular in the world, and it would be a shame to miss them just because you can't get in the water for one reason or another. On the Discovery, you can keep your feet dry and still experience spectacular coral gardens. They offer three trips a day. *Info: Tel. 305-293-0099.*

Dry Tortugas Ferry

This is a great way to get to the Dry Tortugas and Fort Jefferson. The boat is comfortable and fast. Refreshments of the usual type are available. They do one round trip daily. The trip is only about 2 1/2 hours each way, so you have plenty of time to explore the park and go on the tour. Snorkeling gear is provided and the snorkeling is good. *Info: Margaret Street, Key West Seaport. www.yankeefreedom.com; Tel. 305-294-7009.*

ATTRACTIONS

The attractions of quintessential tourist town Key West are almost unending. Some are great. Some are embarrassingly lame.

Audubon House & Tropical Gardens

Run by a non-profit educational organization, the Audubon House is where the famous man hung out and created several of his masterpieces. The house, loaded with antiques, and the gardens are quaint and interesting. Visitors can view 28 first-edition works. For serious birders, this is a holy shrine. It's a very nice, small museum with a pleasant gift shop. *Info: 205 Whitehead Street. www.audubonhouse.com; Tel. 305-294-2116.*

Sunset Pier and Mallory Square

Every evening, just before sunset, a great crowd of remarkable street performers and even more remarkable people selling street stuff gathers to work the great crowd of tourists. It's great. Just about everybody loves it. The sunset can be beautiful. The people watching is some of the best anywhere. *Do not miss the drunken Frenchman who has trained his cats to do tricks*—unbelievable. *Info: Go to the end of Duval Street and follow your nose to the left.*

Harry S. Truman Little White House

This beautiful old home is wonderfully maintained and loaded with historically significant items. The atmosphere is just like it was in the old days. Guides schooled in the most trivial of Truman trivia lead informative tours. The tour I was on included a real Truman nerd who tried hard to stump the guide. Couldn't be done. *Info: 111 Front Street. www.trumanlittlewhite house.com; Tel. 305-294-9911.*

Ernest Hemingway Home & Museum

The main attraction here is the cats with too many toes. The Hemingway cats have been inbreeding for so long they have little oddities (like too many toes) that endear them to the tourist public. The house is full of memorabilia. The 75 + cats are mostly in the garden. The museum is open every day of the year.

SPORTS & RECREATION

Info: 907 Whitehead Street. www.hemingwayhome.com.

Old Town Trolley

The trolley starts out in Mallory Square and runs around all over town with nine stops throughout the tourist-oriented parts of town. You can get on and off all day once you buy a ticket. This is a good way to get a look at the town and decide where you want to spend your time. It costs the same as the Conch Train – $25 for adults and $12 for kids – but you can use it all day. *Info: Tel. 800-213-2474.*

Conch Tour Train

The 90-minute tours on the cornball Conch Train take in the main points of touristic interest in town. Tickets are $25 for adults and $12 for kids. Kids love it. They have a

HIGH GAS PRICES

Almost everything costs more in the Keys. Gas and diesel fuel are hauled down to the Keys on the same long, slow road you drive down on. The extra trucking distance costs money and you, the buyer, have to pay it. Expect to pay about 25 cents more per gallon for your gas in the Keys.

ticket booth in Mallory Square. *Info: Tel. 800-213-2474.*

Key West Aquarium

I've been coming to the Aquarium since I was eight years old, and I still love the place. It's very far from being a big-time multi-media aquarium with albino sperm whales, but it is a good exhibit with its own Old Key West Charm. The shark cage out back is always a hoot. Over the last fifty years, I've visited dozens and dozens of times. Kids of all ages love it. *Info: Whitehead Street. Tel. 800-868-7482.*

Wild Dolphin Adventures

This excursion takes you snorkeling just offshore in places where those frisky wild dolphins come to play. These guys are not in cages. They're not going to let you scratch 'em on the tummy and ride along holding onto a fin, but they do get close enough for you to appreciate just how free and athletic they really are. *If you want to mess around with dolphins, this is the way to do it.* Skip the roadside dolphin attractions. *Info: Tel. 305-296-3737.*

GOLF

Key West Golf Club
Green fees at this plain, public 18-holer run around $175 - too much, considering the condition of the greens. Key West is hot, so consider an early-bird special or an evening round. Of course that's when most of the other thinking people want to play. The Keys are not really a golfing destination but, if you simply *must* play, this is your deal. *Info: www.keywestgolf.com; Tel. 305-294-5232.*

BEACHES, PARKS & ECO-WALKS
Although nothing like the famed beaches of Fort Lauderdale or Panama City, there are a couple of great beaches in Key West. Some have coconut palms and sand. Due to the protective reefs offshore, there is no surf of any significance.

C.B. Harvey Rest Beach Park
This is a small, sometimes quiet beach with little to do but wade about and look at the seascape. Great! It's at the end of White Street.

Clarence S. Higgs Memorial Beach
This is a big beach with all the

SAND FLEAS

Many Keys beaches feature irritating sand fleas, almost invisible little buggers that swarm around the beach. For some reason they never seem to get any higher than about three feet off the ground, but in that zone they rule. Many people have their favorite sauces to drive away the little ankle-biters but, to my knowledge, none of these spreads works for everyone. Many swear by Avon's Skin-So-Soft, so it's a good idea to bring some as well as the usual high-DEET mosquito repellant.

touristy beach stuff: tennis courts, volleyball, fishing pier, fast food wagons, and a play area with all sorts of bits and pieces for kids. Instead of saying the whole long mouthful of a name, locals simply refer to it as **County Beach**. It's on Atlantic Avenue.

Smathers Beach
Blazingly sunny and convenient to the jet fumes of the airport, Smathers Beach has a few amenities for the public and decent snorkeling.

Fort Zachary Taylor
This park has one of the nicest beaches in Key West. It's a

SPORTS & RECREATION

SPORTS & RECREATION

good sunset beach. If you follow Petronia Street from Duval a couple of blocks, you'll come to the entrance. They offer all sorts of fun things to do, including kayaks and snorkeling gear for rent. *Info: Tel. 305-295-0033.*

GUIDED BIKE & WALKING TOURS

Walking around Old Town with a camera is great but you're missing all sorts of historical details and obscure bits of local color if you don't go with a guide.

Lloyd's Original Key West Bike Tours

Mr. Lloyd leads guided bike tours through the scenic back streets and popular tourist areas of Key West, specializing in keeping kids fascinated. He makes several stops to sample fresh fruit picked from trees along the route. This is the most talked-about tour in Key West. *Info: www.lloydstropicalbiketour.com; Tel. 305-294-1882.*

Trails of Margaritaville

With five bar stops, this is not a tour to take the kids on. Some tour participants never actually make it to the end, dropping out along the way to worship Jimmy in their own fashion. Actually, you need to be a real fan to feel good about paying $20 for this 90-minute tour. The tour leaves everyday from Captain Tony's (not sure why), takes in Jimmy's old Key West house, and ends up (surprise, surprise) at Margaritaville. You need to call ahead for reservations and you have to wear a loud shirt. If you're a die-hard parrothead you might like this. *Info: Tel. 305-292-2040.*

Sharon Wells

Sharon Wells organizes a slew of Key West tours including ghost, gay, literary, nature treks and architectural tours. You can buy the notes for the tours from her web site and do them self-guided at your leisure. *Info: www.seekeywest.com. Tel. 305-294-8380.*

Gay Trolley Tours

Saturday only (12am) you can

hop on the gaily-colored trolley for a short tour highlighting Key West's gay and lesbian culture and history. It's fun and you don't have to be gay—just happy. It lasts a little over an hour and costs $20. *Info: Tel. 305-294-4603.*

FESTIVALS & PARTIES
Parrothead Week
During the first week of November, Buffet fans flock to town for this annual "meeting of the minds" convention. It is a good excuse (do we need another one?) to do the usual: drink, smoke, and walk around looking at everyone else doing the same thing.

Hemingway Days Festival
All things Hemingway are celebrated at this famous festival. Even though the famous author's descendants and estate eschew the event, it remains the premier Hemingway happening. Sloppy Joe's look-a-like contest is perhaps the most famous part of this boozy, fun-filled celebration. *Info: July 17-22. Tel. 305-296-2388.*

Fantasy Fest
Without a doubt, this is the wildest and most fun of all the Key West parties. Costume competitions, parades, street fairs, promenades, grand parades and other excuses for dressing up and drinking to excess are the norm. Clothing is often replaced by extensive body paint. If nudity, public drunkenness and the flaunting of unusual lifestyles make you uneasy, don't come to town during this period. *Info: October 19-28. Tel. 305-296-1817.*

Spring Break
Spring Break is all of March. Wheee!

Conch Republic Days
This celebration includes such outlandish events as bed races, "drag" races and other wacky festivities to mark the anniversary of the Conch Republic seceding from the US.

This is one of the wilder (and funnier) of the annual Key West parties. *Info: April 20-29. Tel. 305-294-2298.*

Pridefest Key West
Gay and lesbian celebration honoring the city's famous openness, freedom and diversity. *Info: June 6-10.*

Key West Songwriters' Festival
This annual showcase for singer-songwriters is sponsored by the Hog's Breath Saloon and features some of the genre's best performers appearing at dozens of small, intimate venues. *Info: May 2-6. Tel. 305-296-4222.*

World Sailfish Championship
Lots of fishing action, parties and VIP invitational parties. *Info: April 17-21. Tel. 305-395-3474.*

Key West House and Garden Tour
This is the best of the open house tours in Old Town. Historic private homes and their exotic gardens are open for public appreciation. Some classic old Key West homes are only available for viewing during this yearly tour. *Info: March 16-17.*

Hog's Breath King Mackerel Tournament
Sponsored by the bar of the same name, this is one of the bigger tournaments of the year. *Info: January 26-28. Tel. 305-797-1117.*

Florida Keys Seafood Festival
Sample seafood specialties from all the best local eateries. Admission is free, but you will need to pay for the best of the goodies. *Info: January 14. Tel. 305-292-4501.*

Key West Old Island Days
Residents open up their charming Old Town homes and gardens to architectural and horticultural aficionados. *Info: Febuary 27-28. Tel. 305-294-9501.*

Key West Craft Show
Info: January 28-29. Tel. 305-294-1241.

Conch Shell Blowing Contest
This is just what it sounds like: an excuse to drink a lot and blow off. *Info: March 3. Tel. 305-294-9501.*

Keys Poker Run
The Keys are a popular destination for bikers all year, but every fall, a huge horde of hog riders roars down the Overseas Highway, ending up in Key West for a small version of Daytona Beach's famous Bike Week. Ask at any cycle shop in the Keys for details. *Info: Mid-September. www.keyspokerrun.com.*

BIKING & SCOOTING
Bikes and scooters are a great way to see Key West as there are not really any long distances to cover. Traffic and booze are the issues. Biking or scooting on Duval, Roosevelt or other main drag is not a good idea. The consumption of alcoholic beverages while biking or scooting is pretty much insane anywhere, but in Key West it's even insaner. Every weekend several scooting casualties are treated in the local hospital. If you must scoot, here are a few places to help you do so. Touts and rental kiosks abound. Rent straight from the major rental places and get a better deal. Some of the touts will bargain a little.

Barracuda Scooters
Right in the center of things. *Info: 2401 N. Roosevelt Blvd. Tel. 305-296-8007.*

Pirate Scooter Rentals
These guys have a good selection of bikes, with plenty for kids. They do pickup and delivery to all the Key West hotels. Bikes run about $15 per day. Scooters go for around $50 for 24 hours. They've also got cute little electric cars that hold several people. *Info: 401 Southard Street. www.piratescooter rentals.com; Tel. 305-295-0000.*

Paradise Scooter Rentals
Bikes and scooters. The scooters run around $25 an hour or $60 for all day. *Info: 430 Duval Street. Tel. 305-292-6441.*

MOTORCYCLING
Rent a Harley at **Bone Island Cycle Repairs**. Keep the noise down - the local cops will bust you for revving up your engine and making a racket. For real. *Info: Tel. 305-293-9877.*

SPORTS & RECREATION

SPORTS & RECREATION

KAYAKING

The shallow, calm water with channels meandering through mangroves and turtle grass flats makes the Keys perfect kayaking territory. There are hundreds of sites where you can easily plop in a couple of kayaks and, moments later, find yourself deep in the wilderness. Kayaking through the mangroves and over the turtle grass flats is one eco-tour all visitors to the Keys should appreciate. This is a good way to get an up-close look at bird nesting sites, sharks, stingrays, sea urchins, crabs, Florida lobsters and all manner of blowfish and other strange critters.

The very best time to enjoy a quiet paddle on the flats is at daybreak or just before dark. This is when a lot of fishy activity begins. It's feeding time for some of the big boys like snapper, grouper, bonefish, sharks and permit. Drifting and paddling slowly around the miles and miles of turtle grass flats is a wonderful experience.

The currents can be quite strong, especially near bridges and in the channels between small keys or sand banks. If

you time things right, you can plan your kayak trips to straddle a change in the tides. You can drift out on the last of the outgoing tide and drift back in when the tide changes and starts to come back in. Try to plan your trips so you drift with the tide instead of fighting against it.

Any trips you make outdoors in the Keys require sunscreen, a hat and drinking water (beer, although also necessary, doesn't count). On a kayak or boat you are soaking up even more sun than usual, because the reflection from the water almost doubles your exposure to the effects of the sun.

Of particular interest is the group of small keys just to the west of Key West called the **Marquesas**. This is a prime kayaking area (*photo below*). **Island Kayak** can arrange the whole schmeer.

Lazy Dog Outfitters
Formerly Hurricane Hole, these guys rent all sorts of kayaks and fun watercraft. If you're into kayak fishing, this is the place. They also arrange a variety of interesting guided kayak tours. *Info: 5114 Overseas Hwy. www.lazydog.com; Tel. 305-295-9898.*

Island Kayak
These guys have basic rentals and offer guided tours. Their 3-hour tour costs $40. *Info: 2400 N. Roosevelt Blvd. Tel. 305-292-0059.*

SPORTS & RECREATION

7. THE EVERGLADES

HIGHLIGHTS

▲ Gators, gators, gators

▲ Exploring the back country by ranger-led tour or kayak

▲ Tour Ten Thousand Islands and see gurgling manatees

▲ Fishing on the flats and in the canals

▲ Wandering interpretive trails through cypress hammocks and sawgrass

COORDINATES

Everglades National Park occupies the entire tip of south Florida and is bordered to the north by the Tamiami Trail, Hwy. 41, to the south and west by Florida Bay and to the east by the Keys. **Everglades City** and **Homestead** are the closest towns.

INTRO

The third largest park in the lower 48, **Everglades National Park** covers about 2500 square miles from Florida's East coast where the Keys start to the West coast right by Marco Island and Everglades City. The park is easily enjoyed by casual visitors who only have a few hours to spend.

The park is accessible through three entrances with modern visitors' centers with ranger-led tours and activities, pontoon boat tours through the backcountry and marked walking and paddling trails allowing tourists to easily explore the park.

Short trails and boardwalks provide drive up, park, and enjoy opportunities for all ages. The park features 156 miles of canoe/ kayak and walking trails.

The **Ernest Coe Visitor Center** is at the east entrance of the park near Homestead. It is located at the edge of the park and the beginning of the long road that stretches through the park to Flamingo.

The road passes trail heads, campground areas, several scenic boardwalks and many places to pull over and admire the desolate beauty of the Everglades. Flamingo visitor's center and the park-run marina are at the end of the road. Pontoon boat and paddling tours leave from there into the back country.

Unfortunately, Hurricane Katrina put an end to the motel and other tourist facilities that used to be there. The large campground at Flamingo is one of the best in the park.

Along the north side of the park, on the Tamiami Trail, is the Shark River Visitors Center. This entrance to the park features a paved, 17-mile long loop road closed-to motorized traffic road into the park.

There is a tram visitors can ride with informative commentary. Bicycles are available for rent.

Near Everglades City, Gulf Coast Visitor Center is the place to board one of the park's pontoon boats for a ranger-led tour of Ten Thousand Islands where you are likely to see manatees, dolphins and other exotic wildlife.

You may not realize it, but as you drive through the upper Keys, most of what you see on the Florida Bay side of the road is part of Everglades National Park. Thousands of small keys and hundreds of square miles of sand and turtle grass flats can be explored in small boats or by kayak or canoe.

The more adventurous can spend as much as a week traveling by canoe or kayak across the wilderness just as early explorers did but with mosquito netting, comfortable bedding and catered meals. Day trips will also do just fine.

Much of the park is only accessible by boat so, if you really want to know what the Everglades is all about, you will need to do some exploring by kayak, boat or canoe.

As the Keys curve underneath the peninsula of Florida, they protect the shallow **Florida Bay**, protected by **Everglades National Park** and **Great Heron National Wildlife Refuge**. Thousands of small mangrove islands are strewn across hundreds of square miles of shallow sand and turtle grass flats. Bonefish, permit, tarpon and snapper swarm. Sharks and rays cruise. Exotic birds shake their tail feathers.

EVERGLADES IN A DAY

A day is just enough time to go get a feel for either the east side of the park, near Homestead or the west end of the park around Everglades City. You can also enjoy the park as you drive across the state along Hwy. 41, Tamiami Trail—the northern border of the park with a visit to **Shark Valley Visitor Center** for a tram ride into the saw grass. You will have time to take a pontoon boat or kayak tour, walk a couple of trails and enjoy boardwalks leading through cypress hammocks. Gators are guaranteed.

SIGHTS

If your plans take you across the state on Hwy. 41, Tamiami Trail, you will be driving along the northern border of the park almost the whole way. As you drive you can stop off at a couple of interesting parts of the park, and, if you plan well, you may have time to take the tram ride at Shark Valley.

Morning

Whichever part of the park you are going to, I suggest you check the park's web site *(www.nps.gov/ever)* to get the schedules for boat tours or other ranger-led activities that you might want to incorporate into your day's activities.

From Homestead, follow Hwy. 9336 to the park entrance.

On your way to the east park entrance, stop at **Robert Is Here** fruit stand for a healthful fruit smoothie. Exotic fruits are their specialty. It's not your average tourist trap—you'll like the place and probably stop again on your way out to buy fruit for back home.

The **Ernest Coe Visitor Center** is worth stopping at to grab a couple of maps and brochures—but not much

more. Next, don't miss the **Royal Palm Visitor Center** and the adjacent **Anhinga Trail**— absolutely the best place to see gators and other wildlife up close.

The visitor center itself has the same brochures and some informative displays. The drink machine always seems to be one of the coldest ones around.

The Anhinga Trail starts at the Visitor Center and is one of the very nicest walks in the park and also has the advantage of being very easy to enjoy—the entire path is either paved or consists of wide boardwalks with wooden

SIGHTS

BURMESE PYTHONS

One of the largest constrictors in the world, Burmese pythons that used to be pets have been dropped off in the everglades and are breeding fast and present a significant threat to the Everglades ecosystem. Rangers are attempting to control the situation. You may likely see some.

rails. It's also one of the closest trails to the park entrance so if you don't have time to drive all the way to Flamingo, don't miss this one.

The trail winds along some small ponds and wetlands choked with bream, turtles, exotic birds and thousands of gators. You get really close to them. Kids will absolutely love the Anhinga Trail. Keep small children close to you.

If you are coming from the west side of the state, I suggest heading straight for the **Gulf Coast Visitor Center** just past Everglades City to check out what tours and guided walks are scheduled. Their trips through Ten Thousand Islands on large pontoon boats are great. You just skirt the edges of the park but you certainly get a good feel for the beauty and wildlife in the area. It's an awesome trip usually including **dolphin** and **manatee sightings**. Lots of birds.

Afternoon

After enjoying the delights of the Gulf Coast Visitor Center and a trip through Ten Thousand Islands, stop at the **Rod & Gun Club** for lunch on their classic veranda under the rotating ceiling fans. I suggest ordering whatever seafood menu item the waitress suggests. This is the romantic old timey restaurant with big white porches overlooking the river your wife has been nagging you to take her to.

Whichever direction you are driving across the state you should stop at the **Shark Valley Visitor Center** and take the **17-mile long tram** ride through the sawgrass. There is a 50-foot tower you can climb, walking trails and lots of gators. The kids will like the educational tram ride (and the gators).

Hwy. 94 is a scenic alternative route through Big Cypress National Preserve that passes through some beautiful cy-

SIGHTS

press hammocks. It is a little slower than taking the Tamiami Trail the whole way but is not really out of the way and the kids will love all the gators.

A WEEKEND IN THE EVERGLADES

For a weekend, spend the first night at either Everglades City or Homestead enjoying **pontoon boat tours, kayaking** and **walking trails**. Saturday afternoon, head to the other end of the park stopping at **Shark Valley** for the tram ride.

Typically, for a weekend excursion through the park, you can spend Friday night at Everglades City, enjoy the Ten Thousand Islands area of the park in the morning and, later in the afternoon, enjoy the drive along the Tamiami Trail towards the east end of the park. Spend Saturday night near the east entrance in Homestead. On Sunday, enjoy trails on foot, by kayak or take a pontoon boat ride into the backcountry at Flamingo.

Friday Night
For a quaint riverside Olde Florida hotel you can't beat the **Everglades Rod & Gun Club** in Everglades City. Tell your wife you are going to take her for that romantic dinner she's been asking for in an old white house with a big porch with ceiling fans overlooking the river. The local seafood in the restaurant is great. The rooms are okay.

Spend the night in period splendor to be ready to get up early in the morning for fishing, kayaking and wildlife viewing.

Saturday
Saturday morning drive down to the Gulf Coast Visitor Center for a ranger-led pontoon boat tour. There are no walking trails at this end of the park—you pretty much have to get out onto the water to see the park.

ALTERNATE PLAN
You can approach the park from either the Everglades City, west end by the **Gulf Coast Visitor Center** or, across the state past the **Shark Valley Visitor Center** on the Tamiami Trail to the east end of the park, near Homestead and the **Ernest Coe Visitor Center**.

SIGHTS

The ranger-led boat ride takes you into Ten Thousand Islands and to the edge of the Gulf of Mexico. The tours take about two hours and you are just about guaranteed to see dolphins, manatees, eagles and all manner of interesting wildlife. The rangers keep up an interesting patter for most of the ride and seem to enjoy questions from the tourists—I guess it breaks up the routine a little.

I suggest a quiet lunch at one of the fish shacks along School Drive or Camilla Street. If **stone crabs** are in season be sure to honk down a couple of lbs.

After stretching your legs here, head west again towards the **Shark Valley Visitor Center** for the tram tour into the saw grass.

The **Tamiami Trail**, Hwy. 41, between Miami and Naples

passes by dozens of interesting places to stop for a short walk and is absolutely filthy with alligators, birds and cool plants to look at. You hardly even have to get out of your car to enjoy the park. But the more you do get out, the more you'll see.

If you have time, turn off the Tamiami Trail onto Loop Road, Hwy. 94. This is a small road, partly paved that heads off along the edge of the park and connects back up to the Tamiami Trail after about 15 miles. It is not nearly as busy as 41 and you will have to drive much more slowly so you are likely to see much more wildlife than you would along Tamiami Trail.

The road is crossed by numerous culverts with water flowing underneath. Stop your car just before these culverts and walk quietly to the small ponds that are usually on either side of the road where you will see hundreds of fish, thousands of gators and millions of interesting birds. Be careful—gators are often resting in the weeds alongside the road. You may end up walking too close to them and not realize it. Small dogs are regularly seized and gobbled up by roadside gators when tourists let their dogs out of the car to pee.

At Shark Valley, there is a 17-mile long loop road with several walking trails leading off of it. The road passes mostly through saw grass with a few interesting hammocks and some old borrow pits filled to overflowing with alligators.

At the Visitor Center you can buy tickets for the tram or rent bicycles. The tram ride is great with interesting commentary from the ranger and plenty of slowing down for photographs. About halfway is a 50-foot tower you can climb up for panoramic views.

Airboat rides are also a possibility. They are crude fun but still fun. Think jet skis, zip lines, bungee jumping, and snow mobiles. Lots of fun zooming loudly around smashing down saw grass but don't expect to see much wildlife other than fleeing birds no matter what the tour operators say.

I suggest checking into one of the comfortable hotels near Homestead and indulging in some of the *muy autentico* Mexican food available here.

Sunday

You really need the whole day for the east end of the park. The **Anhinga Trail**, near the park entrance, is not to be missed. You should plan on visiting **Long Pine Key** and a couple of other walking trails along your way to Flamingo.

Take a pontoon boat tour from Flamingo or book and afternoon fishing on the flats and back in the mangroves. There are many reliable charter captains and flats guides in the area. You can also rent a kayak from the Flamingo marina for a self-guided paddle or go on a ranger-led kayak tour.

I particularly like the **Eco-Pond Loop** walking trail by the Flamingo campground. I usually surprise myself with how many bird species I can see in just a few minutes. Watch out for alligators here.

SIGHTS

SIGHTS

A WEEK IN THE EVERGLADES

With a week, you can take your time enjoying both ends of the park as well as having a good time along the Tamiami Trail counting alligators.

You can start your park exploration from either the Everglades City, west side or the Homestead, east end of the park with the Tamiami Trail in between.

Everglades City & Ten Thousand Islands

Most of the park in this area is hard to enjoy without getting out on the water. **Ten Thousand Islands** is made up of enormous areas of mangroves with a myriad of small inlets and estuaries. The bay is mostly shallow grass and sand flats with winding channels and fast-running tides.

The easiest and perhaps best way to see this area of the

park is to go on a pontoon boat tour from the Gulf Cost Visitor Center right by Everglades City. The large, stable boats are comfortable, shaded and suitable for families with kids as well as us grey-haired generation. You can park your car just a few feet from the boat, hobble aboard and have a solid look at what Ten Thousand Islands is all about.

The tour guides keep up an educational talk as you move out into the mangroves and through channels to the edge of the Gulf of Mexico. Manatees, dolphins, rolling tarpon, gruesome gators, eagles and all sorts of other interesting swamp and sea critters are fairly common sightings.

If you want to get waaay back into the swamp and catch some fish, book a day or two with Captain Dave Prickett. If redfish, snook, tarpon and maybe a sea trout or two for the pan interest you, a day spent in a small boat with a reliable guide will be a day you and your kids will remember for your lifetimes. I seriously recommend a full day fishing in the Everglades, and Chokoloskee, near Ever-

SIGHTS

glades City, is probably the best place to do it.

Another way to see the best of the Ten Thousand Islands part of the park is by kayak. **Everglades Area Tours** takes paddlers along with kayaks in power boats to fairly remote parts of the park before shutting off the engines and launching the kayaks. These guys get you to out-of-the-way areas for quiet paddling. They can arrange all the details for multi-day paddling trips or kayak fishing expeditions. On their one day trip, you get to do some beachcombing on beaches so remote only birds and turtles will be your companions.

In the Everglades City area, there are two great places to stay. I always enjoy the **Ever-**

glades City Rod & Gun Club with its quaint Olde Florida charm and wonderful local seafood served under swirling ceiling fans. The **Ivey House B&B** is also a nice place to stay and can arrange all sorts of interesting back country explorations.

If you must, do an **airboat ride** (*see photo above*). They are thrilling and some can even be educational. Kids love 'em. There are several airboat tour operators that run through the Barron River and over some private land near the park. Airboats are not actually allowed into the park.

Shark Valley & The Tamiami Trail
There are no walking trails at the west end of the park but, on the Tamiami Trail, east

about 15 miles past the turn to Everglades City is the wonderful **Kirby Storter Boardwalk**, part of **Big Cypress National Preserve.**

This is a half mile-long, wandering boardwalk snaking around through cypress hammocks and small sloughs in the area called **Georges Strand**. It is an easy walk. With luck you will see eastern bluebirds or a tufted titmouse. The photo opportunities are tremendous at sunrise and sunset especially.

If you are driving across the state on the Tamiami Trail, Hwy. 41, you are going to drive right past the **Shark Valley Visitor Center** with a 20-mile tram ride and several cool walking trails. This is a nice way to see into the heart of the park without having to even stretch your legs if you don't want to. It's also a good place to stop for a real leg stretch if you want to bike the trail or walk any of the walking trails. Kids will like this one.

The food at the restaurant by the entrance is pretty lame.

A nice scenic alternative to part of the Tamiami Trail is to take Hwy. 94 that runs through Big Cypress National Preserve. You will want to drive slowly and stop off to see and photograph the cypress hammocks.

There are several places where culverts pass under the road with small ponds stuffed with gators. Be careful here: gators are often resting in the grass and underbrush right by the edge of the road. You might not realize you at close until the gator rushes off (or attacks you) with a roar.

Brought your fishing pole and license didn't you? You will pass by dozens of great places to pull over and throw your hook in. There are lots of places for children to get fishing fever. I grew up fishing the canal alongside the Tamiami Trail and never got over it.

Ernest Coe, Royal Palm & Flamingo Visitor Centers

The Ernest Coe and Royal Palm Visitors Centers are both close to the east entrance to the park, near Homestead. Route 9336 leads right into the park, past both Visitors Centers and on down to Flamingo and the Flamingo Visitors Center and marina.

It is an easy day to make the drive to Flamingo stopping at three or four walking trails on the way. Several places in the park offer ranger-led tours of various sorts that include educational talks. These are well worth doing. Always check the park web site in advance for scheduled activities. *Info: www.nps.gov/ever.*

Starting at the Royal Palm Visitor Center, the **Anhinga Trail** is without a doubt the coolest trail in the park. It is all paved or boardwalk so it is easy to walk. The boardwalk passes over some rootsy-looking swamp areas loaded, absolutely loaded with alligators, fish, turtles and birds.

This is the top gator-viewing spot in the world and one of the top birding spots in North America. Enjoy. The kids will love it but keep them close since alligators frequently cross the paths or lurk in the tall grass nearby.

Pa-hay-okee Overlook is a short boardwalk with a raised area for viewing out over the saw grass and hammocks. I

like watching the big vultures that always seem to be hanging around.

Long Pine Key walking and biking trails total many miles of fairly basic dirt paths through pine barrens, hammocks and some dryish areas of saw grass. You can get maps at the Visitors Centers. You will need them.

The **Eco Pond walk** by Flamingo campground is one of my favorites. This is also one of the top gator, croc and bird viewing locations anywhere.

Flamingo marina offers several ways for visitors to enjoy the remote, back country parts of the park in relative comfort.

The pontoon boat tours are well worth the time and cost. They go well back into the mangroves and give visitors a glimpse of what the park.

A remnant of the Cold War, right in the middle of Everglades National Park is a mothballed Nike Missile Site. The nukes are reportedly gone and the Park Service recently decided to offer tours to the curious public. They have proved so popular the additional tours have been added. Check the park web site for tour times and meeting locations. You drive your own car in a caravan of visitors led by a ranger to the site gates. Tours usually leave from the Royal Palm Visitor Center. *Info: Tel. 305-242-7700.*

BEST SLEEPS & EATS

HOMESTEAD AREA

In Homestead you have the usual lodging choices available at any interstate off ramp. There are a couple of mildly interesting non-chain places. The Hampton Inn is by far the most comfortable lodging in the area. But plastic.

There are some wonderful restaurant choices. Ribs, seafood and especially Mexican food are all well done in the area.

Best Western Gateway to the Keys $$

The last motel on the mainland, this is a standard medium-priced lodging with coffee maker, small refrigerator and simple breakfast served in the lobby. It is a reasonable budget option. *Info: 411 S Krome Avenue. Tel. 305 246-5100.*

Everglades Int'l Hostel, Inc. $

Fairly standard hostel offer with dorms and private rooms. You can rent bikes here and do some local exploring. Beds start around $15. *Info: 20 SW 2nd Avenue, Florida City. www.evergladeshostel.com; Tel. 305-248-1122.*

Grove Inn Country Guest House $$

Close to Everglades National Park and Key Largo, Grove Inn is one of the few B&Bs in the area. It is comfortable and friendly. The area nearby is home to some of the largest and most important botanical gardens in the US. Orchid growers flock to the area and you can tour some. They do a nice breakfast featuring local fruits. *Info: 22540 S.W. 177 Avenue, Redlands. www.groveinn.com; Tel. 305-247-6572.*

Hampton Inn $$$

What's to say about a Hampton? They probably have the best mattresses in Homestead and their wi-fi actually works quite well in the rooms. As usual they do the high end motel thing quite well. The location is convenient to the park and for enjoying the local sights and dining. *Info: 124 E Palm Drive, Florida City. www.hamptoninnfloridacity.com; Tel. 305-247-8833, 800-426-7866.*

Redland Hotel $$

Not your usual HoJo's, the Redlands still offers all the services and amenities of the chains but with their own quaint style and old-timey atmosphere. The bedrooms feature gauze curtains and period bedspreads. Very romantic. The building dates to 1904 and has been, over the years, a hotel, dry goods store, post office, library, and rooming house. Their location is good for short trips to the Keys and Everglades. *Info: 5 South Flagler Avenue, Homestead. www.redlandhotel.com; Tel. 305 246-1904, 800-595-1904.*

Robert Is Here Fruit Stand $$

If you have come this far in Florida you have passed hundreds of fruit stands selling all the usual plastic alligators and bags of oranges. Stop at this one. It's a landmark. They have an always interesting, colossal array of fruit and vegetables and make the same into won-

derful smoothies. *Info: 19200 SW 344th Street, Homestead. www.robertishere.com; Tel. 305-246-1592.*

SLEEPS & EATS

Redland Rib House $$

I try to eat here whenever I drive by even if I'm not hungry at the moment. You can wear shorts, T-shirt and flip flops and get sauce all over yourself. It's all about ribs. Extra napkins please! *Info: Coconut Palm & Krome Avenue, Homestead. Tel. 305-246-8866.*

Rosarita's $$

Not a chain but a very Mexican seeming Mexican restaurant, beef tongue tacos and other *autentico* items lurk on the menu. All things that involve green chili are good here. *Info: A couple of blocks off Highway 1 on the road to the Coe Visitor Entrance to the park.*

EVERGLADES CITY / TEN THOUSAND ISLAND AREA

Perhaps because there is no interstate off ramp nearby, there are no chain motels in the area. This is good allowing a couple of good mom and pop places to survive and even thrive. One really great monument to Olde Florida, **The Everglades City Rod & Gun Club** retains its quaint charm.

Everglades City offers several places to honk down fresh local seafood—from waterside fish shacks to Olde Florida charm dining on long white porches overlooking the river with ceiling fans circling romantically overhead. This is where you get your gator bites.

BEST OF THE BEST NEAR EVERGLADES NATIONAL PARK
Everglades City Rod & Gun Club $$
This is probably my favorite place to stay on the mainland. I never get tired of the heavy *Olde Florida* ambiance with moldy stuffed boar heads and yellowing tarpon of preposterous size mounted on the smoke-stained walls. The old ceiling fans still turn over the dining tables on the veranda overlooking the river.

The air conditioned rooms are simple and clean and not what you would call modern but, since the whole place drips with so much charm, this can be forgiven. The old white buildings with wrap-around porches, the lobby and restaurant make me feel like I am in some sort of Bogart movie. Celebrities by the score have left their spoor here. You can sleep in the same beds that Barron Collier, Roosevelt, Eisenhower, Babe Ruth and other notables slept in. In the restaurant, order whatever local fish is happening. Ask the waitress. Last time I asked she said "Pompano. My cousin Billy was out pampanoin' yesterday and it's good." It was. I love this place. *Info: Everglades City. www.evergladesrodandgun.com; Tel. 239-695-2101.*

Captain's Table Hotel $$

Nice but basic motel with, regular rooms, junior suites and villas, restaurant, boat ramp, gas, bait and slips. They have a nice pool. *Info: 102 East Broadway, Everglades City. www.captainstablehotel.com; Tel. 239-695-4211.*

Everglades City Motel $-$$

The basic traditional motel has been nicely remodeled. They have some units with fundamental kitchen facilities. This is one of the better bargains in the area. *Info: Hwy. 29, Everglades City. www.evergladescitymotel.com; Tel. 239-695-4224, 800-695-8353.*

Ivey House B&B $$

This B&B has sprung a new wing with modern rooms with all the latest amenities. It's very comfortable. Some older rooms share a bath. They have a nice pool and offer a good but simple breakfast. They arrange for some of the best guided trips in and around the park. They have wi-fi in the rooms. Ivey House is justifiably proud of its Florida Certified Green Lodging designation. *Info: 107 Camellia Street, Everglades City. www.iveyhouse.com; Tel. 239-695-3299.*

SLEEPS & EATS

SLEEPS & EATS

GATOR BITES

Hanker to try some gator? Many restaurants in the area offer fried gator tail—usually deep fried nuggets. They are really not much different from chicken fingers. Kids love 'em.

Everglades City Rod & Gun Club $$

This is not fine dining by any stretch of the imagination. The long white porch overlooking the river is the definition of a romantic dining experience. Add the ceiling fans and the knowledge that Mick Jagger, Hemingway, Kate Moss and other luminaries sat their butts in the same chairs yours is in.

The thing they do well here is local seafood—most of the rest of the food comes off the Sysco truck. Ask the waitress what's good. Don't order salmon or those deep fried scallops they sell at Captain D's. Get pompano, snapper, grouper, local flounder and crabs. Sometimes they have wonderful fresh shrimp **but be sure to ask**—they might serve you the deep fried, factory-breaded shrimp like you get at Shoney's. *Info: Everglades City. www.evergladesrodandgun.com; Tel. 239-695-2101.*

The Seafood Depot $$

At the Captain's Table Hotel – usual stuff. It's actually inside the old train depot from days gone by. Cool. *Info: 102 East Broadway, Everglades City. www.captainstablehotel.com; Tel. 239-695-4211.*

City Seafood, Café, Market $-$$

Nice waterside location for fresh fish, crabs and beer. Not fancy but the fish and crabs come off their own boats. This is a great place to honk down stone crabs. *Info: 702 Begonia Street, Everglades City. Tel. 239-695-4700.*

Camilla Street Grill $$

This is a funky, waterside crab shack with the usual seafood, BBQ, hush puppies, she crab soup, herb salad, and, of course, grouper They have live music from time to time. *Info: Camilla Street, Everglades City. Tel. 239-695-2003.*

Triad Seafood Café & Market $

And yet another dockside seafood shack. In addition to the all-you-can-eat stone crab deal, these guys have sandwiches, home-made soups and chowders, key lime and peanut butter pie. Ask for mullet. Open only for lunch. *Info: School Drive, Everglades City. Tel. 239-695-2662.*

Backcountry Cafe $

This is the place to eat breakfast. The local guides and wags start hanging out here and telling lies very early. If you listen closely, you may find out who's catchin' what and how. They serve crab for lunch and dinner and will pack you a lunch. I like the place. *Info: 305 Collier Ave, Everglades City. Tel. 239-695-2552.*

BEST SHOPPING

The **Homestead area** near the East end of the park has all the American-style malls and chain stores/restaurants you could possibly hope for. There is a Wal-Mart.

Everglades City and Chokoloskee on the west end of the park have meager shopping selections: a small grocery, minimart/liquor store and a great bait shop.

Souvenir shopping is limited to the stuffed alligator-type trinkets you can find in any Florida gas station/convenience store/fruit stand.

In Everglades City, there is a small grocery store and the wonderful True Value.

True Value is a great little tackle shop advertising "Tackle, Ammo, Knives." You might need all this. In case the kids are getting bored, they have a good selection of non-lethal things for children.

SPORTS & RECREATION

BEST SPORTS & RECREATION

Kayaking and canoeing through the back country is not to be missed. You can do this on your own through the many well-marked paddling trails or go with a guided small group. This is not the same as an airboat trip!

Getting way off the road in the swamp where the only sounds are the wind in the cypress trees and saw grass, birds chirping, frogs croaking and gators bellowing is an unforgettable experience—one of the best Everglades National Park things to do.

Fishing in Everglades National Park is some of the best in Florida. I grew up in Miami and wasted many a day wandering around the Everglades along canal-lined dirt roads catching brim and catfish on worms with cane poles. Flats fishing from small boats is some of the best anywhere.

Scuba diving and snorkeling can be done in Florida Bay but there is not much in the way of coral reefs and most visitors would be disappointed.

The road from the east entrance of the park to Flamingo winds past numerous boardwalks and marked walking trails. Many are wheelchair accessible and all offer visitors an easy way to see the park's glories.

Boat tours led by park rangers are one of the easiest, most comfortable and best ways to get well into the Everglades and see most of the things that make it famous. They leave from the Gulf Coast Visitor Center near Everglades City and from the marina at Flamingo on regular schedules.

FISHING

The Everglades and waters around it are wonderful for fishing. I highly recommend getting a fishing license and keeping a simple fishing rig in the car at all times. There are zillions of bridges, ponds, canals and mangrove inlets that you drive right up to, park and casually fish for a few minutes or all day.

The Ten Thousand Islands area is famous for fishing for redfish, snook, tarpon and other beauties. For this area, it is almost essential to go with a guide, in their boat. Local conditions include tricky navigation and shallow oyster beds waiting to chew up outboard props. A good guide will be fishing almost daily and know what's biting, where and on what kind of bait. There are many reliable charter captains and flats guides in the area.

The Tamiami trail is lined with canals teeming with brim, bass, catfish, gar and gators. Look for side roads to explore. There are often small ponds near culverts worth wetting a line in. Look for gators though. Seriously, these small ponds sometimes have hundreds of alligators of all sizes lurking about. Some areas are so gator infested it is a waste of time to try to fish in them. Unless you want to catch a gator.

Fishing guides in the Homestead area can take you either flats fishing in the Florida Bay area of the park fishing for redfish, tarpon and permit or poking through mangrove estuaries looking for snook and redfish.

Captain Doug Lillard
Specializing in fly fishing, Captain Doug trailers his flats skiff and launches as close as he can to the places most likely to produce permit, tarpon, snook, sea trout and the like. He is active in South Florida especially in Florida Bay. *Info: www.floridaflyfishing.com; Tel. 941-232-2960.*

Captain Benny Blanco
Available for half-day to week-long charters, Captain Benny promises glimpses of crocodiles, alligators, porpoise, manatees, eagles, osprey and sharks on the way to catch snook, tarpon, trout, redfish, grouper, tripletail, cobia and mackerel. That's a long list of fish but he delivers—it might take the whole week though. *Info: www.fishingflamingo. com; Tel. 305-431-9915.*

Guides around Chokoloskee and Everglades City specialize in hooking up redfish, snook, tarpon and sea trout in the winding mangrove inlets around Ten Thousand Islands.

SPORTS & RECREATION

SPORTS & RECREATION

Captain Dave Prickett

I first went fishing with Dave Prickett about 30 years ago. He's still doing it and still full of it. He put me on some huge redfish in places where I didn't think there would be *any* fish at all. "Cast right there" he'd say. There are other guides in the area for sure, but you really should spend a day with Captain Dave Prickett. *Info: Chokoloskee. Tel. 239-695-2286.*

Captain Bill Lindsay

Another area old-timer, Captain Bill uses spinning, fly and bait casting, as clients prefer, to help them land snook, tarpon and redfish as well as other species such as such as barracuda, sea trout, various types of jack, tripletail, sharks, jewfish and cobia as available. *Info: Chokoloskee. www.chokoloskeefishing.com; Tel. 239-695-0314.*

AIRBOAT RIDES & ATTRACTIONS

Airboat rides! You will see dozens of signs urging you to blast through the swamp on airboats. They are undoubtedly fun and operators swear the noise of the engines, etc. does not actually scare the wildlife. "They get used to the noise." Whatever.

There are two areas the tours go through. Most of the airboat tours on the west side of the park run mostly on water through mangroves and also along the Barron River. Tours more to the east tend to run over saw grass plains visiting hammocks and along man-made canals. You can ask what type of terrain your operator will be visiting.

No airboats are allowed in Everglades National Park so all the rides you see advertised are on private land *near the park.*

Most of the boats charge around $50 per person. You may want to call ahead. During busy times, you may not be able to just drive up and hop on the next airboat heading out. Reservations are usually accepted. The best type of ride to take is in one of the smaller boats holding a maximum of six people. Tour bus-sized airboats herd tourists through the swamps like cattle.

Expect to see lots of gators, a few of the braver birds and, possibly, a manatee or two. Kids love airboat rides.

Are airboats bad for the environment? Airboats are not allowed in any part of Everglades National Park. Tour operators say the wildlife gets used to the incredible noise (they use airplane engines with little or no mufflers) and that airboats don't have underwater propellers to make hamburger out of manatees.

Not all the birds and animals run or hide from the airboats so you will see some on almost any trip but, many animals, especially the shyest ones will completely avoid areas where airboats regularly run.

Ecologists say manatees suffer from getting hit by airboats even if the boats don't have underwater propellers. Sediment in shallow areas where airboats run gets disturbed and ruts form where airboats travel disturbing the natural order. Tour operators and enthusiasts say they are fun. They are fun. They certainly ain't *good* for the environment. For a better feel for the Everglades, try a kayak tour instead.

Turtlemom Abacon

Southern Florida is where the whole concept of "tourist trap" was created in the first place. Beginning with the incredibly cheesy casino at the corner of Krome Avenue and continuing past Indian villages, gator parks and air boat rides all the way to Naples, there is no shortage of tourist traps along Tamiami Trail. Don't miss these tourist hotspots:

Everglades Alligator Farm

A nice day out for the kids. Airboats run on canals around the farm. A bit off Hwy. 41, plan on spending several hours if your kids like snakes and gators and things like that. *Info: 40351 SW 192nd Ave., Florida City. www.everglades.com; Tel. 305-247-2628.*

Capt. Jungle Erv's Airboat Rides

On Hwy. 41 just west of the turnoff to Everglades City,

Captain Jungle Erv offers airboat rides through saw grass prairies, mangrove and cypress swamps, pinelands, and hardwood hammocks. Most of the rides are along the Barron River where you can also experience marine and estuarine environments. *Info: Hwy. 41, Everglades City. www.jungleervairboatworld.com; Tel. 877-695-2820.*

Capt. Doug's Small Airboat Tours

The one-hour tours of Everglades River are done in six-person airboats. I don't know how many boats they have but you can basically just show up at almost any time and zoom off with little, if any waiting. *Info: Everglades City. www.captaindougs.com; Tel. 800-282-9194.*

Wooten's

If you have a need to see caged gators, snakes, bears, raccoons and other creatures from the swamp, this is the place to do it. Located on the Tamiami Trail five miles east of the turn to Everglades City, Wooten's "sanctuary" also sells cold drinks and airboat rides. Swamp buggies are also fun and this is the place to try it. Some of their tours run within Big Cypress Preserve. Kids generally love the place. *Info: Tamiami Trail. www.wootenseverglades.com; Tel. 239-695-2781.*

Captain Doug's

Gator park and Indian Village all in one, this is your basic gator/bear park selling cold drinks, chips, air boat rides and glimpses of a weird "Indian Village". Stop for a drink. *Info: Everglades City. Tel. 800-282-9194.*

BIRDING

Birders twitch with anticipation at the thought of visiting the famed Anhinga Trail (**sora, smooth-billed ani, least bittern** and **great white heron**) which is where many of the

photographs you see in bird magazines have been taken. Few places in the US hold the interest of birders as does the Everglades.

With over 300 species year round, your best chance of sighting a **roseate spoonbill** (*see photo on previous page*) or a **purple gallinule**, and certainly adding significantly to your life list, is a visit to Everglades National Park. 347 species have been identified within the park.

Nine-Mile Pond is another famous birding site. Expect to see short-tailed hawks, osprey, herons, bald eagles and, glory that they are, roseate spoonbills.

West Lake is where to look for American widgeon, ruddy, pintail, shoveler, scaup (lesser and ring-necked) and teal (green and blue-winged). White-crowned pigeons are seen in the afternoon over the lake. American coots swarm in huge numbers.

Some species you can expect to see in the park are wood stork, mottled duck, red-breasted merganser, swallow-tailed kite, red-shouldered hawk, snail kite and seaside sparrow.

RANGER-LED PROGRAMS

Rangers give talks, guided walks, provide commentary on pontoon boat trips and lectures on wildlife and ecological issues of the park. **Canoe adventures**, **bird walks**, **tropical botany walks**, and **croc talks** are included. Check the park web site or call the main park number for listings. Program subjects and program times change with the seasons. *Info: www.nps.gov/ever/ planyourvisit/rangerprograms. htm; Tel. 305-242-7700.*

RANGER-LED BOAT TOURS

Completely different from airboat rides, both the Flamingo Visitor Center and the Gulf Coast Visitor Center offer trips through the backcountry and Ten Thousand Islands on large, comfortable pontoon boats.

This is well worth doing if you have no other way of getting out into the park. It looks a little touristy, and it is, but the tours are designed to pass through the most interesting areas and near where wildlife is easiest to see. The rangers know what they are

SPORTS & RECREATION

talking about and seem to welcome questions. I've done all the tours at both ends of the park and love it.

The boats are quiet and the rangers quite informative as they keep up their patter about the park and the sights you're seeing. These tours are the best way to get a feel for the park with complete comfort. The schedules are available at the visitors' centers.

Pontoon boats leave from the marina at Flamingo on a set schedule. Check the park website for seasonal times. The boats are large with padded seats and awnings. The ranger spends most of the trip commenting on passing wildlife and things of interest. The trips head up into the park mostly away from Florida Bay.

Ten Thousand Islands is a part of the park that you just can't

visit by car or on foot and the ranger led pontoon boat tours are perfect for most visitors.

The large pontoon boats head out through the edge of Ten Thousand Islands to the edge of the Gulf of Mexico and Florida Bay. You see birds by the thousands, manatees, dolphins, and alligators. Eagles are often seen on this tour. At one point in the tour, you can actually see the condos of Marco Island off in the distance. *Info: Flamingo Marina: Tel. 239-695-2945. Gulf Coast Visitor Center: Tel. 239-695-2591.*

WALKS & TRAILS
There are miles of foot trails in the east end of the park. Most start at the road that runs from Ernest Coe Visitor Center to Flamingo. There are signs on the highway and parking. Many are boardwalks and easy to get to and enjoy— just a short walk from the car. One of the best in the park, the **Anhinga Trail** starts at the Royal Palm Visitor Center.

Anhinga Trail
This is probably the best walk in the park and is very easy to enjoy due to the asphalt and wooden walkways. You are

certain to see dozens of alligators and interesting birds.

Birders claim this as one of the top spots in Florida for bird watching and there are thousands swarming around. From huge buzzards to egrets and anhingas and zillions of LBBs (little brown birds).

Pa-hay-okee Trail

This is a boardwalk with a small raised platform for looking out over the saw grass. The walk goes through a small hammock and offers pretty much the same view you get from a car as you drive along. I usually see gigantic vultures hanging around waiting for me to do something wrong. It's a nice place to stretch your legs and enjoy the silence.

Eco Pond Loop

I always enjoy this short walk near the campground. If you look closely you may see a couple of crocs—look for a narrower snout than the typical shovel-nosed alligators. It's a great spot for bird photos with plenty of wading birds, songbirds and ducks.

Long Pine Key

Abandoned roadbeds and trails form a 43-mile long network of paved and primitive trails through the pinelands. These are great for long, leisurely walks. A couple of the trails are open to bikes. The Long Pine Key picnic area provides access to the trails.

There are no hiking trails or boardwalks into Everglades national Park near the Gulf Coast Visitor Center but there are a couple of great ones nearby at Fakahatchee Strand Preserve and Big Cypress National Preserve off the Tamiami Trail.

SHARK VALLEY TRAM TOURS

Leaving from the Shark Valley Visitor Center just off Hwy 41, Tamiami Trail, guided, two hour tram tours take visi-

SPORTS & RECREATION

SPORTS & RECREATION

tors on a 15-mile loop into the saw grass swamps of the Everglades. About halfway along is a 50-foot tower (*see photo on previous page*) that you can climb for a view of the famous "River of Grass." Rangers keep up an informative patter as you ride along. The tram does not stop along the way except at the observation tower.

The rangers do a good job describing what you are passing and pointing out wildlife you would probably not notice otherwise. This is definitely worth doing, especially if you have kids. You will be sure to see some big gators, raccoons, egrets, and other critters.

Alternatively, you can rent bikes at the Visitor Center and do as much or as little of the loop on your own. This way you get to stop and check out some of the walks that branch off into the swamp. But you give up the commentary from the rangers if you do your own thing. *Info: Shark Valley Visitor Center. Tel. 305-221-8455.*

BIKING
Bicycling is a wonderful way

to see the quiet beauty of the park up close. Bikes are allowed on all the main roads in the park including Shark Valley. You can also ride on the Old Ingraham Highway, Long Pine Key Nature Trail, Snake Bight trail and Rowdy Bend.

The Shark Valley Visitor Center rents bikes for the two to three hour loop road. Near the Visitor Center, park your bikes and walk the Bobcat Boardwalk and the Otter Cave Hammock trails that go through tropical hardwood islands. *Info: Shark Valley Visitor Center. Tel. 305-221-8455.*

Long Pine Key on the road to Flamingo has several long bike trails through the pinelands.

KAYAKING & PADDLING
Kayaking is hip. Kayaking is cool. Kayaking is the new yoga, or tofu, or something. Kayaking in Everglades National Park is about as sweet as you can get. If you only have time to do one particular thing in the park and want get at least a basic feel for what the area is all about, go on a kayak tour.

For day trippers, **Halfway Creek, Turner River, Sandfly Island** and **Ten Thousand Islands**, among other places, offer marked trails.

There are several places you can rent equipment and set out on your own through well-marked paddling trails or go on specialist guided tours for a couple of hours or for a week or two.

The Wilderness Waterway Trail

Running from the Gulf Coast Visitor Center through the heart of the park to Flamingo, the water trail is used by canoers, kayakers, and power boaters. There are small camping areas with minimal facilities at strategic points along the 99-mile long trail. It takes most people about eight days to do the whole thing. Outfitters can arrange everything except sunscreen, mosquito repellant and your iPod. If you are an experienced paddler and outdoor explorer, you can set out on your own.

Florida Bay Outfitters

If you want to do the whole Wilderness Waterway Trail or just a day trip from Flamingo, these are the guys to go with.

They can arrange everything for the eight day to two week trip. All you'll need to bring is hat, sunscreen and lots and lots of mosquito repellant. *Info: Key Largo. www.kayakfloridakeys.com; Tel. 305-451-3018.*

Flamingo Visitor Center

The marina at Flamingo rents single and tandem kayaks, small skiffs and canoes. They offer guided kayak trips or you can set off on your own. *Info: Flamingo Visitor Center; Tel. 239-695-2945.*

The Ten Thousand Islands area of the park is a wonderful place to explore slowly and quietly by canoe or kayak. There are numerous places to launch and the most interesting parts of the area are close by. There are dozens of places to rent equipment or sign up for a naturalist-led tour.

Everglades Rentals & Eco Adventures

This is probably the oldest outfitter in the area having been in business for over 30 years. *Info: 107 Camellia Street, Everglades City. www.iveyhouse.com; Tel. 239-695-3299.*

SPORTS & RECREATION

SPORTS & RECREATION

Saltwater Sports

With multiple locations, Saltwater Sports is one of the largest rental operations in the area. They claim no reservations are needed at any of their rental locations. Kayaks are their specialty and they offer sit on singles and doubles as well as single and double sea kayaks and fishing kayaks all set up and ready to go. They will do deliveries. *Info: 11369 E. Tamiami Trail, Naples. www.saltwatersportsflorida.com; Tel. 239-262-6149.*

Everglades Area Tours

Their most popular tour by far is a naturalist-guided **Boat Assisted Kayak Eco Tour** that takes even inexperienced paddlers to remote parts of the park by boat where they board kayaks to quietly get you close to wildlife. The trip is topped off by a walking tour to explore the tidal zone of a remote island beach. The company also offers a wide variety of other tours as well as the usual rentals. *Info: 238 Mamie Street, Chokoloskee Island. www.evergladesareatours.com; Tel. 239-695-3633.*

8. PRACTICAL MATTERS

ARRIVALS & DEPARTURES
Flying to Florida
If you're flying commercial, your choices are Miami and Key West. The airport in Marathon is used for charter and private flights only.

Miami International Airport is a big, stinky old airport. After arrival, get into your rental car and get out on the road quickly. The area around the airport is not salubrious and should be avoided. Wait until you get to Homestead to do your shopping for vacation essentials. Prices will be lower, and you won't get caught up in all the Miami traffic. See *Getting There*, below, for tips on the best routes out of town.

Key West controls the **Florida Keys Marathon Airport**. Key West would, of course, prefer that visitors to the Keys, along with their money, would land in their town rather than in Marathon. Landing and gate fees in Marathon are high and airlines have trouble making a profit since they must charge so much. For this reason, the Marathon airport usually has no scheduled commercial service.

Key West International Airport is on the opposite end of the island from the action of Old Town and Duval Street. It's too far to walk. You'll need a taxi. *Info: Roosevelt Boulevard. Tel. 305-296-5439.*

These are the main carriers serving Key West:
- **American**, *Tel. 800-433-7300.*
- **Delta**, *Tel. 800-221-1212.*
- **Continental**, *Tel. 800-525-0280.*
- **US Air**, *Tel. 800-428-4322.*

Charter Airlines
- **Air Key West**, *Tel. 305-923-4033.*
- **Florida Coastal**, *Tel. 888-435-9322.*
- **SeaCoast Airlines**, *Tel. 866-302-6278.*
- **CapeAir** - *Tel. 508-771-6944*

Cruises
Key West is an ever-popular cruise destination. Water sports, cool bars, snazzy restaurants, gay lifestyles, T-shirt shops—what

more could a cruiser ask for? A wide variety of cruise lines include Key West in their itineraries. Cruise ships usually arrive in port in the morning and leave by late afternoon, so taking a cruise will give you no more than a rushed glimpse of the Keys.

Try one of the following:
• **Carnival**, Tel. 888-CARNIVAL, www.carnival.com;
• **Royal Caribbean**, Tel. 305-341-0204 .www.royalcaribbean.com;
• **Celebrity Cruise Line**, Tel. 800-722-5941. www.celebrity.com;
• **Disney Cruise Line**, Tel. 800-951-3532. www.disneycruise.com;
• **Norwegian Cruise Line**, 866-234-7350. www.ncl.com;
• **Radisson Seven Seas Cruises**, Tel. 877-505-5370. www.rssc.com.

GETTING TO THE KEYS

If you know the best route, you can get out of the Miami airport and be on your way to the Keys quickly. If you take the wrong route, you can spend a couple of hours in heavy traffic cussing your luck. Also, the area around the Miami airport can be dangerous (a few tourists have been robbed and murdered after getting lost), so you need to know how to get out of the area quickly and get on down to the Keys without delay.

From the airport, immediately get on Route 826 west. You then need to get on the Florida Turnpike. Route 836 connects Route 826 and the Florida Turnpike about 8 or 10 miles south of the airport. You can stay on the Turnpike (toll road) all the way to the end in Homestead if you like, or take the Tamiami Trail to connect with Krome Avenue (which is free but slower) all the way to Homestead.

I grew up in Miami and love it, but I still encourage a quick exit if it is not your travel destination. Get directions from your rental car agent for the most direct route from the parking lot to **Route 826 west**. This leads to **Route 836**, which is a connector to the Florida Turnpike.

Avoid US 1 until you have to get on it in Homestead. To get out of Miami and down to the Keys quickly, the **Florida Turnpike** is the quickest way, but there is a toll. A couple of miles further west, **Krome Avenue** pretty much parallels US 1 and the Florida Turnpike, and is fairly fast and free. You can get onto Krome Avenue by heading west on the Tamiami Trail. It's also quite a scenic drive, passing tropical nurseries and old Florida-style fruit stands.

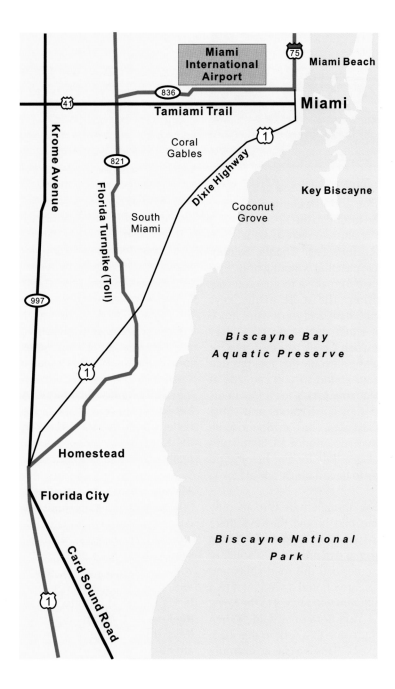

A little past the end of the Turnpike, and just before you get to the turnoff to the Keys, you have a chance to refresh yourself at **Skeeter's Last Chance Saloon**. Just past that watering hole, you have to make a momentous decision. The route to the Keys splits here, and you have a choice of either staying on US 1 over **Jewfish Creek** to Key Largo, or taking the route that goes through Card Sound so you can stop at **Alabama Jack's** for a few beers or rum concoctions and some crab cakes. The Card Sound route involves a minor $1.50 toll and takes a little longer, but you do get to have a quick one at Jack's.

Even though there is really only one road through the Keys, there are two ways to get to Key Largo from the mainland. Just south of Homestead the road splits and you are offered a choice of two different ways to get to the Keys. As Yogi Bera once said "When you come to a fork in the road, take it." This is a classic example

of that dilemma. If you continue on US 1, you'll get there a little faster and pass through some mangrove swamps and small fishy-looking bays such as **Lake Surprise**. You get to go over the politically incorrectly named **Jewfish Creek**, which is the official start of the Keys. The roadbed you drive on used to be the famous Flagler's famous railroad line from Miami to Key West. You'll see this old abandoned rail line over and over again as you drive down through the Keys.

If, on the other hand, you take the route to the Keys that goes through **Card Sound**, the drive will take you about 15 minutes longer and you'll have to pay a small toll. You see pretty much the same swamps and sunny bays but you get to stop at one of the better places to have a drink in the Keys (even though it's not really quite in the Keys).

Alabama Jack's is a roadside, open-air bar and grill where you can enjoy your favorite hot weather beverages, grouper sandwiches and conch chowder while gazing at passing manatees, crocs and gators. Alabama Jack's is a good introduction to the Keys, and is fairly typical of Keys drink emporiums. There are no doors or windows. Bring your bug spray inside with you—you'll probably need it.

Enjoy Jack's. If you don't, turn around and head back to Miami, because the vibe at Alabama Jack's is very much the vibe you can expect at most of the Keys' better drinking establishments.

Drive Slowwwww! The speed limit on the Overseas Highway is, for the most part, 55 mph, with a few areas of 45 mph and some school zones down to 30 mph. The road has long stretches with only two lanes, and there are few good places to pass. The highway is lined with small businesses, attractions, motels and other roadside urban stuff and there is a lot of local traffic. Hurrying on the Overseas Highway is rarely possible and never a good idea. Radar traps are common.

On holiday weekends (Labor Day, Memorial Day, etc), traffic in the Keys becomes unbearable. On the first day of the long weekend, it's bumper-to-bumper in the southbound lanes, all the way from Homestead to Key West. On the last day of the weekend, the same parking lot convenes in the northbound lanes.

If you must drive here on a holiday weekend, allow triple or quadruple the usual driving time.

GETTING AROUND
Getting around the Keys is straightforward—there is only one main road. The Overseas Highway is the road into, through, and back out of the Keys. It runs spectacularly from Homestead to Key West.

CAR RENTAL
Renting a car offers the maximum in flexibility, except in Key West where parking is a hassle and almost everything is close enough to walk to anyway. In the rest of the Keys, a car is essential, because almost nothing is within walking distance of anything else and the heat in the sun can be brutal.

Car rental agencies can be found at the airports. Book ahead.

Upper Keys
- **Enterprise**, *Ocean Reef Club. Tel. 305-367-5972.*
- **Just Jeeps**, *Islamorada. Tel. 305-367-1070.*
- **Budget**, *97300 Overseas Highway, Key Largo, Tel. 305-852-7416.*

Middle Keys
- **Budget-Rent-A-Car**, *Marathon. Tel. 305-743-3998.*
- **Enterprise Rent-A-Car**, *Marathon. Tel. 305-289-7630.*
- **Just Jeeps Of The Keys**, *Marathon. Tel. 866-587-8533.*
- **Avis Rent A Car**, *Marathon. Tel. 305-743-5428.*

Key West
- **Alamo**, *Tel. 305-294-6675.*
- **Dollar**, *Tel. 305-296-9921.*
- **Electric Cars of Key West**, *Tel. 305-295-7777.*
- **Enterprise**, *Tel. 305-451-3998.*
- **Hertz**, *Tel. 305-294-1039.*
- **Hummer Dune Buggy Rentals**, *Tel. 305-292-4868.*
- **Key West Cruiser**, *Tel. 305-294-4724.*
- **National Car Rental**, *Tel. 305-294-6675.*

TAXIS
Upper Keys
- **Islamorada Taxi**, *Tel. 305-664-4100.*

Middle Keys
- **Action Taxi**, *Tel. 305-743-6800.*

- **Cheapo Taxi**, *Tel. 305-743-7420.*

Lower Keys
- **Courtesy Taxi & Delivery**, Tel. 305-872-9314.
- **Sunset Taxi**, *Tel. 305-872-4233.*

Key West
- **A Airport Cab Co.**, *Tel. 305-292-1111.*
- **Friendly Cab Comany**, *Tel. 305-292-0000, 305-295-5555*

BUSES
There is limited bus service in the Keys. Real estate is quite expensive in the Keys, so many tourism workers live in Homestead and commute to work. Greyhound runs two buses daily from Miami to Key West with numerous stops along the way. The trip takes about 6 hours. *Info*: **Greyhound Bus Lines**, *Key West International Airport. Tel. 305-296-9072, 800-229-9424.*

Another good way to get there and back again is **Keys Shuttle**. These guys run a service from Miami International and Fort Lauderdale to wherever you are going in the Keys. They run every two hours, and charge about $100 for the full trip from Miami to Key West, which takes about four hours. *Info: Marathon. Tel. 305-289-9997.*

BASIC INFORMATION
Climate & Weather

The Keys have two main seasons. Trade winds blow pretty steadily during the summer, keeping things reasonably cool. Summer afternoons often see squalls move in for a couple of hours, cooling things down considerably.

From November through March temperatures can get into the 60s but the skies are almost always clear and blue. Locals think they need to stay inside near the fire. Visitors from almost anywhere else think the weather is perfect.

The rest of the year, temperatures are mild and the trade winds liven things up, although it can get hot and muggy. Flat calm seas often occur this time of year at dawn and sometimes dusk. That is a magical time to be out on the water.

Realistically, hurricanes are possible from June through October. If you are visiting during that time, keep your ears open for warnings. The authorities try to move all visitors out of the Keys well in advance of hurricanes.

The average annual temperature is a balmy 80°F. The Keys receive 40 to 45 inches of rain each year.

TEMPERATURES

January	70°
February	71°
March	73°
April	77°
May	80°
June	82°
July	84°
August	85°
September	83°
October	79°
November	74°
December	71°

Emergencies & Safety

As is true all over the US, 911 gets you connected to emergency services.

- **Fisherman's Hospital**, *MM 48.7, Marathon. Tel. 305-743-5533.*
- **Lower Keys Medical Center**, *Stock Island. Tel. 305-294-5531.*
- **Mariner's Hospital**, *MM 91.5, Plantation Key. Tel. 305-853-3700.*

As you would anywhere, take common precautions. Murders, rapes and robberies are not common in the Keys. In 2005, Key West experienced one murder, 3.9 rapes (?) and 48 robberies. Not bad for a bustling tourist town.

Underage drinkers are jailed overnight, set to picking up trash on the streets in an orange jump suit for the next day, then let go. You'll probably see some of these orange jump-suited young people during your visit. You've been warned.

Here are a few travelers' tips:

Never leave anything of value in an unattended car. You're asking for trouble if you leave things out in plain sight.

Don't wear a fanny pack. I know all the other tourists strap them on as soon as they leave home but these are magnets for rogues using razor blades. I suggest a money belt that straps on around your waist under your shirt.

Don't walk around alone late at night. Nuff said.

Don't leave your drink unattended. Someone might drop a roofy in, drugging you into an easy mark.

Some T-shirt shops on Duval Street advertise seemingly great deals, such as 10 T-shirts for $10. This is not going to happen. They simply want you to come inside, where they can try to cajole you into a more lucrative (for them) purchase. Sometimes, in the noise, bustle and loud music, punters only realize after they left the shop that the actual price they paid for their T-shirts was more like $15 each.

If you must smoke pot, do not do it in public. Key West is a party town but it is not wide open (yet).

Etiquette

The Keys are waaaay laid-back. Key West is famous as a party town where people get much looser than they tend to back in Ardmore.

All of this is true, but it does not give you a license to be rude or stupid. You can't run around the streets naked, you can't smoke dope in public, and you can't drink in the streets and go around shouting "wooooo!" all night. Actually, there are some guesthouses and hotels where you can do these things, but do them in private if you must do them at all.

During **Fantasy Fest**, some of the rules seem to be relaxed a little. It is not unusual to see people walking or bopping down the street dressed only in artfully done body paint. This can be beautiful. It can also be grotesque. The cops seem to ignore it unless things get out of hand.

Food & Eating Out

The **selection of restaurants is great**, with something for everyone. Funky Cuban cafés compete with fancy-shmancy drizzly-sauce fusion places serving seafood with the very latest of west coast/Pac rim/mojo sauce-smothered grouper cheeks. Or whatever. There are a couple of wonderful hole-in-the-wall joints where steaming hot fresh seafood comes to you on waxed paper. Delicious!

You can get excellent seafood in the Keys if you know where to go (which you will as soon as you've finished reading this book). However, there are hundreds of mediocre (or worse) restaurants tempting tourists with plastic décor and overpriced frozen seafood that has nothing to do with Florida. Look for a funky place with local license plates in the parking lot, and stick with local specialties like yellowtail.

Conch and lobster are local favorites. The large "Key West" shrimp should be fresh and local (smaller generic "shrimp" may come from farms in Central America). Yellowtail snapper is an excellent local fish ("red snapper" is not red, definitely not local, and probably not even snapper). A wonderful local staple is the fish formerly known as

RESTAURANT PRICES	
$	$5 or less
$$	$5-$8
$$$	$8-$12
$$$$	$12-$25
$$$$$	Over $25

Prices quoted are for the average prices of entrées on the menu.

dolphin. In order to avoid confusion with the marine mammal of the same name, *coryphaena hippurus* (a delicious, firm white fish) is now generally referred to as mahi mahi (or dorado).

$$$ indicates the average prices of entrées on the menu.

Health

The Keys are a healthy place. Most health problems visitors encounter have to do with overindulgence in the things that make the Keys so much fun: sun, booze and food.

Drink lots of water when you are out in the sun. Beer and Cokes won't do the trick—they just make things worse.

Avoid buying cigars on Duval Street unless you smoke them regularly. Dozens of novice cigar smokers barf up their dinners into the gutters of Duval Street every night.

Use big-time SPF sunscreen. Out on the water, the power of the sun's rays are almost doubled due to the reflection from the water.

Don't touch anything underwater. Stinging coral, sea urchins, crabs, stingrays, sharks and all manner of toothy critters await your touch with poisonous spines at the ready.

Hotels

Although there are few true budget options in the Keys other than camping, there is a good variety of lodging. Key West is famous for its quaint B&Bs, Little Palm Island is one of the most luxurious resorts in the world, and the rest of the Keys are noted for waterfront resorts catering to anglers, divers and nature lovers. Although not dirt cheap, there are a few nice, clean and interesting less expensive lodging choices as well. A few well maintained, mom and pop-style motels are left over from the fifties, and make good budget vacation choices.

Internet Access

Even though they are at the end of nowhere, the Keys have good Internet connections.

Most hotels and guesthouses offer wireless connections to guests.

Newspapers

The Keys have a couple of decent local papers. Check out their web sites or subscribe for a month or so before your trip to get in the proper Keys mood. The *Miami Herald* is widely available. The main papers in the Keys are:

- **Islamorada Free Press**, *www.keysnews.com;*
- **The Keynoter**, *www.keynoter.com;*
- **Key West Citizen**, www.keysnews.com;
- **The Reporter**, *www.upperkeysreporter.com;*
- **The Weekly Fisherman**, *www.weeklyfisherman.com;*
- **Key Largo, Islamorada Times**, *www.keystimes.com.*

Time

The Keys are on Eastern Standard Time and change to Daylight Savings along with everyone else.

LODGING PRICES

$	Backpacker: $50 or less
$$	Budget: $50-75
$$$	Midrange: $75-150
$$$$	First-class: $150-250
$$$$$	Luxury: $250 and up

Prices quoted are for one double room.

Tipping

Good service should beget good tips. That's the American way.

Just as anywhere in the US, you should tip according to your satisfaction with the service provided. Not much tipping goes on in Keys hotels unless someone schleps your bags around. Restaurant servers expect 15% and 20% in the upscale joints or more if they do an outstanding job. Some people say the price of the wine or tax should not be considered when figuring the tip. This would seem petty to me if I were a waiter.

Fishing guides and charter boat mates get tipped anywhere from $20 to $100 or more. Check with the boat captain for advice if you are unsure. On party boats, I usually tip the mate $5 or $10.

Tourist Information

I find the Chambers of Commerce in the Keys to be quite useful. They have racks full of those cheesy tourist brochures for area attractions, hotels, restaurants, etc. They can help you sort out what you want to do and how to do it. For instance, they will refer you to fishing guides' associations for lists of guides.

In the Upper Keys contact:
• **Key Largo Chamber of Commerce**, *MM 106 BS. Tel. 305-451-1414.*
• **Islamorada Chamber of Commerce**, *MM 82.4, Islamorada. Tel. 305-664-4503.*

In the Middle Keys contact:
• **Marathon Chamber of Commerce**, *MM 53.5 BS. Tel. 305-743-5417.*

In the Lower Keys contact:
• **Lower Keys Chamber of Commerce**, *MM 31 OS, Big Pine Key. Tel. 305-872-2411.*

In Key West contact:
• **Key West Chamber of Commerce**, *Mallory Square. Tel. 305-294-2587.*

Websites

Be careful of information found on the web. Sites can be waaay out of date. Be sure to call for the latest prices and schedules.

• **Islamorada Free Press**, *www.keysnews.com*
• **The Reporter**, *www.upperkeysreporter.com*
• **The Weekly Fisherman**, *www.weeklyfisherman.com*
• **Key Largo, Islamorada Times**, *www.keystimes.com*

- **Florida Keys On-line Guide,** *www.florida-keys.fl.us*
- **Florida Keys Diving,** *www.flkeysdiving.com*
- **The Florida Keys,** *www.floridakeys.com*
- **Florida Keys Tourism Council,** *www.fla-keys.com*
- **Fishing Listings,** *www.flkeysfishing.com*
- **Key West Parade,** *www.keywest.com*
- **Everglades National Park,** *www.nps.gov/ever*

INDEX

Things Change!
Phone numbers, prices, addresses, quality of service – all change. If you come across any new information, let us know. No item is too small! Contact us at :

jopenroad@aol.com
or
www.openroadguides.com

TravelNotes

TravelNotes

TravelNotes

PHOTO CREDITS

The following photos are from wikimedia commons: p. 20: Aquaimages; p. 30: Clay Degayner; p. 76: Thuresson; p. 97: Andrejs Jegorovs; p. 6 top right: Sandford Brown; p. 56: Marc Ryckaert. *The following photos are from Jeff Shelar/catch-em-all.com:* pp. 6 middle left, 14, 87. *The following photos are from Bruce Morris:* pp. 22 left, 136, 137, 155, 163, 168, 170. *The following photos are from Abyss Dive Center courtesy of Betty Crosley:* p. 25, 86. *The following photos are from istockphoto.com:* pp. 8, 113: cdwheatley; p. 120: JenDen2005; p. 6 bottom: skynesher; p. 197: Elerium. *The following photo is from Florida Keys Wild Bird Rehabilitation Center:* p. 54, 105. *The following photos are from Seaplanes of Key West:* pp. 102, 191. *The following photo is from the Key West Harry S Truman Foundation:* p. 115. *The following photo is from the Theater of the Sea:* p. 53. *The following photo is from The Turtle Hospital:* p. 89. *The following photo is from John Schwarz (www.birdspix.com):* p. 90. *The following photo is from the Ernest Hemingway Home and Museum:* p. 165.

The following images are from flickr.com: front cover: cayobo; back cover: Bogeskov; p. 1: David Berkowitz; p. 5: Kilaana; p. 6 top left: ruthmarie; p. 7 top: DioMakr; p. 7 bottom: cogito ergo imago; pp. 17, 22 right, 24, 29, 73, 82, 198, 206: Stig Nygaard; pp. 3 left, 103, 121: Barbra Kates; p. 9: tylerdurden1; p. 10: Monica R.; pp. 13, 219: Joshua Whitman; pp. 12, 124: placesaroundfl (www.placesaroundflorida.com); p. 16: porkfork6; p. 31: Joe Shlabotnik; pp. 32, 67: Tom Purves; p. 34: Brian Wilson; p. 36: Elin B; p. 37: Innes M. Keighren; p. 39: Marko Budisic; p. 40: Michael S. Smith; p. 46: CaptPiper; p. 47: phault; p. 48: mattk1979; p. 62: greenacre8; p. 63: NOAA; p. 71: DR Ranch; p. 85: Captain D; pp. 88: Zach Klein; p. 91: Mangrove Mike; pp. 37, 92: Viewoftheworld; p. 93: MigRodz; p. 96: PattiSchmidt; p. 101: John Schweitzer; p. 111: Andy Cross; p. 119: djrue; p. 122: paleololigo; p. 123: totobotteri; p. 126: sanjoyg; p. 129: efleming; p. 130: Versatile Aure; p. 131, 135: Steve Weaver; p. 133: stannate; pp. 139, 146: jennmonroe; p. 141: J. Todd Poling; p. 147 bottom: Donna Cote; p. 150: Arawak812; p. 151: The Lost Wanderer; p. 153: szlea; p. 157: jiashiang; p. 158: milan.boers; p. 161: gshowman; p. 169: justthatgoodguyjim; p. 173: b_nicodemus; p. 174: chaunceydavis818; p. 177: bunnygoth; p.180: Sebastian Barillot; p. 183: Bruce Tuten; p. 192: lightninglandon; p. 195: turtlemom4bacon; p. 196: kashyap_hc; p. 199: jmgold; p. 207: Allie_Caulfield; p. 214: plumandlion.

Open Road Publishing

Open Road has launched **a greatl new concept in travel guides** that we call our *Best Of* guides: matching the time you *really* have for your vacation with the right amount of information you need for your perfect trip! No fluff, just the best things to do and see, the best places to stay and eat. Includes one-day, weekend, one-week and two-week trip ideas. Now what could be more perfect than that?

Best Of Guides

Open Road's Best of Arizona, $12.95
Open Road's Best of The Florida Keys & Everglades, $12.95
Open Road's Best of Las Vegas, $14.95
Open Road's Best of New York City, $14.95
Open Road's Best of Southern California, $14.95
Open Road's Best of Northern California, $14.95
Open Road's Best of The Bahamas, $14.95
Open Road's Best of Belize, $14.95
Open Road's Best of Costa Rica, $12.95
Open Road's Best of Honduras, $14.95
Open Road's Best of Panama, $14.95
Open Road's Best of Guatemala, $9.95
Open Road's Best of Ireland, $14.95
Open Road's Best of Italy, $14.95
Open Road's Best of Paris, $12.95
Open Road's Best of Provence &
    The French Riviera, $12.95
Open Road's Best of Spain, $14.95

Family Travel Guides

Open Road's Italy with Kids, $14.95
Open Road's Paris with Kids, $16.95
Open Road's Caribbean with Kids, $14.95
Open Road's London with Kids, $12.95
Open Road's Best National Parks With Kids, $12.95
Open Road's Washington, DC with Kids, $14.95

Order now at: www.openroadguides.com